The Spiritual Secrets of Happiness Health and Success

A Powerful and Practical Guide for Manifesting the Life You Truly Desire

Andrew C. Walton

The Spiritual Secrets of Happiness Health and Success
All rights reserved

Copyright © 2009 by Andrew C. Walton

No part of this publication may be reproduced, stored in a retrieval system, or transmitted in any form or by any means, electronic, mechanical, photocopying, recording or otherwise, without the prior written permission of the author, nor be otherwise circulated in any form of binding or cover other than that in which it is published and without a similar condition being imposed on the subsequent purchaser.

ISBN-10: 1-4421-2527-6
ISBN-13: 978-1-4421-2527-8

Printed in the United States of America

For my Father

Being the Master of your Self is
Being the Master of Your Destiny
True Happiness and Success
Your Assured and Just Rewards

— Andrew C. Walton

CONTENTS

Message to the Reader — 1

About the Author — 3

Introduction — 7

Chapter

1 The Happiness Illusion — 9

2 True Happiness — 15

3 Awakening to Happiness — 25

4 The Spiritual Secret of Manifesting – Experience Your Divine Essence — 39

5 How to Access the Power of Manifesting — 49

6 The Secret Spiritual Formula for Success — 61

7	The Secret Keys to Your Happiness and Success	81
8	Harmony in Everyday Living	93
9	The Start to a Great Day	113
10	Messages from Your True Self	121
11	A New Way of Living	127
12	A Magical Life of Happiness and Effortless Success	137
13	Eight Spiritual Secrets of Good Health	145
14	From Chronic Pain to Good Health – My Miraculous Journey	157
15	Life's Free Spiritual Gifts	165
16	A Wonderful Life	177

MESSAGE TO THE READER

I am an ordinary guy who like nearly everyone else, always wanted to live a truly happy, healthy and successful life. However in my thirties I realized that my life, like that of many others was *not* how I had hoped it would be. I suffered with chronic pain, inner unrest and unhappiness, had not found true love and the moderate financial success I had achieved was paid for through long hours of work, anxiety and worry.

An amazing series of events then occurred through which the spiritual secrets and truths of life were revealed to me. These secrets and revelations form the basis of this book. The power of these secrets miraculously healed me after suffering over twenty five years of chronic pain, brought an enduring level of inner peace and happiness, the loving relationship of a soul mate and the financial prosperity of nearly one million pounds or approximately one and a half million dollars. This book is your invitation and step by step guide to access this same power, the power for you to create a life of true happiness, health and unlimited success.

I would ask you to please keep an open mind as you read, whilst remembering that as human beings we have all been given the gift of free will to accept and act only on those things we currently feel comfortable with and which resonate within us at some level.

Although my personal path to good health included amongst other things the withdrawal of medication this can of course be dangerous. I would therefore strongly advise all readers to consult with their doctor prior to stopping any medication they are currently taking.

If I may take this opportunity to personally wish *you* my friend, a truly wonderful life and trust that these universal secrets will in fact reveal to you just how amazing you really are.

Wishing you love, happiness, health and success.

Andrew C. Walton

ABOUT THE AUTHOR

I am now 46 years old and currently live in the United Kingdom with my partner Charlotte. In addition to writing I run a successful property business providing homes for families. I also have a passion for sport, particularly tennis which I enjoy playing three to four times a week. I now choose to work only when I wish to, usually two or three days a week for eight or nine months of the year, spending the remaining three or four months in the warmth of the beautiful southern coast of Spain.

My Spiritual Journey

From the age of fifteen I suffered from a severe form of facial Neuralgia of which the symptoms were constant acute pain in the left jaw, around the left eye and in the roof of the mouth. The symptoms grew worse throughout my twenties until the age of twenty-eight when I was prescribed a cocktail of strong tablets to control the pain. Throughout my thirties I was taking a daily total of ten tablets, which although reducing the pain, left me feeling constantly tired. I was referred to a number of medical specialists for treatment of the condition and was eventually diagnosed as suffering with Atypical Facial Neuralgia of which I was told there was no known cure.

When I was aged thirty-nine my father was diagnosed with a terminal illness and this proved to be the catalyst for my *transformation on to a spiritual path*. At the age of forty I was still taking a cocktail of prescription pain relief tablets and still experiencing constant pain. However, whilst lying awake in pain in my bedroom during the early hours of one morning I had a revelation so strong it made me jolt upright in bed. The message I received was, in order to be healed of the pain I had suffered with since the age of fifteen, I was to stop taking one half of the drugs I was currently taking for pain relief.

Although at the time this made no sense to me, as the drugs had been the only things that had reduced the pain, the message was so strong that I decided there and then that this was what I would do. I immediately stopped taking half of the drugs and although I knew that it was potentially dangerous to suddenly stop taking strong drugs I believed this was the right thing to do. Although I subsequently suffered withdrawal symptoms for a few months the pain immediately began to disappear.

Within a couple of years I had stopped taking all of my painkillers and miraculously no longer suffered with any pain. The revelation I had in bed that night had proved to be true. *Although various specialists had offered no cure I had nevertheless been healed.*

One year following the original revelation, life continued to be helpful towards me through the bringing together of myself and Charlotte, a soul mate and partner. We both felt a strong connection followed by a growing love. Together we have loved, laughed and shared our life's journey over the last six years. As further revelations with regard to spiritual truths were received in a similar way to the first I started to live life less and less from my ego self and more in accordance with these spiritual secrets. In addition I also started to study numerous spiritual texts and to practice meditation on a regular basis.

Over the last six years I have increasingly lived life according to the spiritual truths revealed to me which have manifested for me a level of inner happiness, peace, love and contentment which I could previously never have hoped or imagined were possible.

These secrets or truths healed me after suffering over twenty-five years of chronic pain, brought the love, laughter and sharing of a soul mate and helped manifest financial prosperity for myself. Above all else the secrets or truths which were revealed to me, and which you will learn of in this book, have brought me *freedom*. Freedom from being a slave of the thinking mind, to let go and live more in the happiness of the present moment, in the happiness and joy of life itself. More freedom from the conditioning of the past or worrying about the future. Freedom to forgive, accept, connect and love. *Freedom to live and create in happiness. Freedom to manifest the life I desire.*

INTRODUCTION

Thank you for choosing this book and in doing so giving yourself the opportunity to experience a deeper and lasting happiness together with the power to easily and effortlessly attract into your life the people, situations, money and success that your heart desires.

The currently accepted norm in our society appears to be that in order to be happy you firstly need to have success. And in order to achieve success it will take much effort, working very hard for long hours whilst making a number of sacrifices along the way. It is also understood that in order to achieve success you will invariably have to endure plenty of worry, anxiety and unease and therefore ironically unhappiness.

The spiritual secrets that you will read of in this book will reveal to you that this hypothesis is in fact *incorrect*. Once you are aware of and follow these secrets you will enjoy a deeper lasting happiness, love and joy in you life *right now.* You will also access the power to start attracting unlimited success easily and effortlessly. You are able to manifest and live the life that you have always desired.

The first part of this book explores what happiness actually is, how to find it, and how to experience it. In order to reveal this I explore and reveal the *happiness illusion* sold to and bought into by nearly everyone in our society.

The second part of this book reveals how you can create the life that you truly desire, whilst enjoying and experiencing a deepening and enduring happiness. I will show you that whatever success you desire for yourself, whether it is career success, business success, sporting success, relationship success, or any other kind, it can be attracted into your life easily and effortlessly.

The third part of this book reveals the spiritual secrets for enjoying good health and how to transform yourself from having poor health to good health using my personal experience as a practical example of this power of transformation.

The reason this book was written was that I felt a strong calling and even destiny to write it. I realized that these truths were revealed to me, not for me to keep to myself, but for them to be shared with whomever may ask. *This book is in your hands, you have therefore asked and all will be revealed to you, as it was for me.*

Chapter 1

❧

The Happiness Illusion

Everyone is looking for something and everyone wants to be happy and successful.

But what is happiness? And what is success?

Most people believe success leads to happiness. There are of course many outwardly successful people in this world who have worked hard and attained wealth, celebrity and status and it appears on the surface that these people have it all and are truly happy. However when you look closer these people still have feelings of insecurity and unhappiness. They have attained the worldly success that our society had conditioned them into believing would make them truly happy, and yet, for many outstandingly successful people once they have achieved these things they may often still find themselves restless with a background feeling of unease, mild anxiety or worse.

It would therefore appear, generally speaking, that there are two ways in which unhappiness is experienced. It is experienced by those who do not have, as yet, what they believe they want. Moreover it is also experienced by those who have attained everything that our society and therefore they themselves believed were needed and desired in order to be happy.

Most of us are so busy trying to do and achieve the things we believe will make us happy that we do not in fact *stop and question* whether the generally accepted hypothesis for experiencing enduring happiness is in fact correct.

Is it true that the things our society and the world promise will make us happy, actually result in happiness for us?

If this is not so, then nearly everyone is mistaken by busily and desperately trying to attain those things, situations, objects, partners, friends, wealth and status that we believe will result in enduring happiness. As no matter how successful we are in attaining things we still cannot seem to experience the treasure that we really want, which is the feeling of lasting peace, joy, happiness and love.

This is of course not to say that people do not have short periods when they feel happiness and love, but these are ephemeral, they do not last for long before unease, boredom, worry or restlessness returns. This therefore cannot be true happiness and joy as it does not last for any extended period, it is fleeting.

True happiness does not regularly change to unhappiness, worry, restlessness, anger and boredom. *It is however possible to experience true happiness now* and once it has been experienced to access the power of manifesting within yourself. You can start to experience this power to create out of true happiness whether you are young or old, currently rich or poor, attractive or not, healthy or unhealthy.

Chapter 2

✥

True Happiness

We are all able to experience true happiness right now, happiness within that does not rely on external success. Once we understand that *true happiness is not reliant on worldly success* we will have been freed from the happiness illusion. We can then start to take life less seriously and begin to *access the power within true happiness*. To access the power to create or manifest anything we wish for in our lives from the position of true happiness. We are then able to start living life like we have never known before. It is as though we are both the scriptwriter and the star of the movie of our lives. We are able to create and live the life we desire, and just as with a movie, we know not to take life too seriously whilst enjoying each scene as it occurs.

The magical secrets of true happiness can be found where few of us ever thought to look, inside ourselves. When you feel true happiness within, success in the outside world is assured without great effort, force, hardship or sacrifice. Success will come to you with ease. You are able to manifest the life you truly wish to live. You will be experiencing the feeling within which you and everyone else in this world is looking for and this feeling will manifest into the physical world around you. This is the secret of true happiness and manifesting or creating out of happiness.

Once this jewel of true happiness within is experienced, you are able to easily and effortlessly start creating the world around you and start attracting into your life anything you may wish for whether it be people, situations, money or lifestyle.

The question is of course how do we find this true happiness within, which as we experience it and feel it will create in our world more joy, peace, freedom and love, as well as for situations, people, money and anything we desire to start being attracted towards us.

The fact is we do not need to find the happiness within as it is already there, it always has been and always will be. *The secret is to experience it.* The real reason you may not be experiencing it now is that most people in the western world have actually been looking for it in the wrong place! Our society has conditioned us in to believing from a young age that to experience lasting happiness we must *firstly* be successful and productive as defined by our society. We first of all need to have a good job, plenty of money, own a nice house, the bigger the better, have a nice car or two, have a romantic partner, a family, status and respect, to take plenty of vacations, enjoy good health, be able to buy all the objects we want, and have plenty of friends. Ideally we want to be rich and famous and have everything money can buy and we need to take the attaining of all of this seriously if we are to be happy.

Phew! Society has convinced us into believing that the more of the above we have the happier we will be. Clearly though this is not the full truth as the majority of those few who have reached the pinnacle of success, as defined by our society, that is to say the rich and famous still do not experience the inner feeling of true happiness, peace and joy and often feel miserable or worse.

Some even self-destruct, turning to drugs and alcohol to ease the pain and emptiness they continue to feel. *Objects, situations, money and people do not give us a feeling of true happiness and peace.* However once you have found true happiness within, these things can be enjoyed and are indeed attracted to you but your happiness does not rely on them, and neither is it created by them.

One way to begin experiencing true happiness is to start loosening our attachments to things. Too much attachment to people, money, achievements, desires and situations creates a block around true happiness. If we are too attached to anything or anyone that thing or person has the power to make us suffer and indeed will do so. An attachment can be likened to a tossed coin. Sometimes the coin will drop on the pleasure side and sometimes it will drop on the pain side. As a result people are constantly fluctuating between pleasure and suffering. People experience pleasure at times when they get what they want and pain when they do not get what they want. Additionally when people experience pleasure at getting what they want, the pleasure does not last for very long, it is ephemeral.

Take the example of what most people would say was the happiest day of their life, their wedding day. The pleasure of this day soon passes. For most people after a few weeks, a few months or a few years, there will be times that their partner does not live up to their expectations and other times when they do not live up to their partner's expectations. This results either in petty arguments, unease, restlessness, boredom, anger, guilt, resentment or even separation. Alternatively consider how long the excitement and pleasure of getting a new car, new house, new job, new television or new clothes lasts.

To experience true happiness within, which in turn creates and manifests more happiness, peace, joy and success in our outer world we firstly need to loosen our grip on attachments. We will then have the power to manifest anything we want out of happiness and not out of attachments or fear. We are then able to create in abandonment, whilst at the same time not taking the creations too seriously. To be able to loosen your grip on attachments firstly consider and recognize that these attachments often make you unhappy as well as happy. Attachments often make you unhappy, because of course, you are attached to them. You really want them in your life. Your worldly self is attached to them which therefore gives your attachments power over you. You give them the power to make you both happy and unhappy.

Because most people are generally too attached to other people, situations, money and possessions they give them power over themselves. *They do this by constantly thinking about them*. They think about and therefore judge to be good or bad, situations involving people, money or possessions that have happened in the past, are happening now, or that may occur in the future.

People rarely experience the present immediate moment without thought and therefore without judgment. To experience the present moment without thinking and judging is to fully accept the present moment, which is to accept life without judgment, to not be fighting against life. When we are able to do this we are making friends with life, and life will respond by being friendly and helpful towards us. We then live in the flow of life and are not constantly fighting against the flow.

Once we are regularly able to do this the happiness we feel and experience within will dramatically increase and this will in time be reflected in our material world, in our life situation. We are then able to create out of happiness and not out of attachments or fears. We accept life as it is, living in the flow of life, having a detached intention for something to appear in our life and then life helps this to come about.

Past, Present and Future

The past and the future exist only in thought form and the thoughts always happen in the present moment. Whenever we think about the past or future we always think about these in the present moment.

The present moment once we stop thinking, is the gateway to true happiness. As life always takes place in the current moment, we are able to connect with it there, connect with life itself, resulting in the feelings of happiness, peace, joy and love.

True inner happiness can only be experienced in the present moment when the mind is not thinking, judging or labeling. The more we live in the *present moment* when our thoughts are paused the more we will connect to the true happiness and peace within ourselves and the more our world around us will change for the better. It is here in the present moment where we need to have our attention in order to experience what we have been looking for, that which we are all looking for which is a feeling of inner peace, enduring happiness and love.

Chapter 3

Awakening to Happiness

The Nature of Thoughts

The feeling of inner happiness is our natural state and although everyone in the world seeks it, most cannot find it and of the ones that do nearly all are unable to keep it. Most are spurred on, knowing deep down that there is a way although time and time again when they think they have found it, happiness disappears.

The cause of unhappiness is our minds, or to be more precise, the type of thoughts the mind is having at any moment in time. When we are thinking unhappy or negative thoughts we feel unhappy. When thinking happy or positive thoughts we feel surface happiness. However, from the position of our higher selves, which is beyond thought, happiness and unhappiness are like two sides of the same playing card. Two sides of the same thinking mind. If we are unable to stop thinking when we decide to, the happy thoughts that we may be thinking at one point will change to unhappy thoughts sooner or later.

For an exercise try this. Turn off the television or radio and focus on something you are really looking forward to in your life, a vacation for example. As you think about going away on vacation you will probably have happy thoughts. Just keep sitting and thinking and it will not be long before those happy thoughts change to unhappy or negative thoughts as your mind starts to think about perceived problems or worries. These problems may be related to the vacation itself, for example concern about what the weather will be like, that the accommodation will be good, concern about how much it is costing, hoping there will be no delays, thinking about whether your house will be secure whilst you are away, worrying about getting all your work done beforehand, or it may be a different problem entirely which just pops in to your mind.

The mind if allowed to continue thinking without restraint will always, sooner or later, and usually sooner, start creating negative unhappy thoughts resulting in the individual experiencing a background feeling of unease, worry and unhappiness.

The more negative our thoughts are, the unhappier we feel. If negative thoughts are particularly strong we will also experience negative emotions in our body simultaneously. Emotions are a result of strong thought meeting the body and are therefore felt in the body. When strong negative thoughts are present people feel particularly unhappy as they also feel bad in their body due to the negative emotions they are feeling.

So as you can now see, the mind can keep us on a roller coaster alternating between surface happiness and unhappiness. This is due to happy thoughts of the past or future constantly changing to unhappy thoughts. In the same way if a current event is happening or another individual acts in a certain way which our mind perceives to be good we feel happy, and when something is happening which our mind judges to be a bad thing our mind produces negative thoughts which then produces feelings of unease and unhappiness.

The mind therefore reacts to what is happening now to create either unhappiness or happiness depending on how the situation is judged. If nothing is happening now the mind may think about the past or future and will again create happy or unhappy thoughts depending on what is thought about. Unfortunately for most of the time, for the majority of people the mind ends up thinking about worries or problems. One minute we may feel relatively happy and fine. The next minute we find ourselves feeling uneasy, restless, slightly anxious or unhappy. We do so because either a situation has occurred or somebody has acted in a certain way or said something that our mind judges to be undesirable, or alternatively our mind has started to think about something bad that has happened in the past or something undesirable that could happen in the future.

Constantly thinking about the past or future or judging the present is the norm for most people in our society. Because most people are unable to quieten their minds and pause this incessant thinking, it is as if the majority of people are unfortunately sleep-walking through their lives on this earth. The sad result of this is that they rarely experience the real beauty, joy and happiness which life truly has to offer. Life happens in one place only. In order to experience life, happiness and true beauty we need to meet life where it unfolds, where it happens. Life always takes place right now in the present, not in a few seconds time or a few seconds ago but right now. Once we are able to stop thinking about the past or future and to stop judging and commenting on the present we are able to pass through the gateway beyond the mere forms of this world to meet and experience the beauty, joy, peace and happiness that is life.

This is available to you right now. The only thing that is blocking your way to this gateway is your thinking mind. Whenever we are able to pause our mind from thinking we are able to walk through this gateway, to wake up from sleepwalking through life, to wake up to life and to wake up to true joy and happiness.

However without being able to stop thinking when we choose to, and without creating gaps between our thoughts we will continually oscillate between pleasure and pain, happiness and unhappiness.

Realizing Your True Happy Self

You are not only your thinking mind you are more than just your thoughts.

Now I understand that this may come as a big surprise to most people. As I write I can hear some readers thinking that they cannot understand this and that they believe who they are is indeed their thoughts or a combination of their dominant thoughts.

A famous philosopher of the last century Jean-Paul Sartre had a revelation that *The consciousness that says 'I am' is not the consciousness that thinks*.

He had realized that there is the thinking self and there is also the observer of the thinking self. The consciousness that observes thoughts is not the thinking mind. The observer of those thoughts is your higher self, your eternal self, your true self. If you were only your thoughts you would not be aware at a given time that you are thinking. Your only self would be a combination of your thoughts. You would only exist as the worldly self, the ego self, the thinking mind.

It is possible to have thoughts and *at the same time* be aware that we are having thoughts. Many people however have not yet realized that they are indeed both the observer of thoughts as well as the thinker. As such it appears that many people seem to be sleepwalking through their lives. They have very limited power to change their life situation and experiences. They are unable to detach themselves from continual thinking and therefore unable to experience their higher self which would reflect in their experience of life, transforming it from an unhappy one to a truly happy experience.

Once we are able to become the observer of the thoughts we are having, we become aware that we are both the observer of thoughts in this world as well as being the thinker or worldly self. We start to feel a connection to our higher selves, beyond thought, and begin to access true wisdom, happiness and the power to manifest the life we wish to lead in this world.

Once we are able to quieten the mind, to stop

thinking and judging, we are able to experience the world in a different way. We are able to experience the world as the observer or true self. We are able to truly see and experience the real beauty, love and magic in the world. We are able to know ourselves as the consciousness that observes our worldly self, other human beings, nature and all of the objects in this world.

There is the *I* and the *worldly self*. The *I* is the eternal you or higher self which exists before thought, after thought stops and also exists during sleep. The higher self exists before you are born into this physical world and exists after you depart. This is what the mystics and enlightened people of various cultures and civilizations throughout the ages have always pointed to.

The other you is the ego or worldly self. Unfortunately this is the only *you* that many people currently know and experience. This you *is* in fact a combination of your thoughts, beliefs, upbringing and past experiences and conditioning by society and peers. *The worldly you or worldly self is already creating the world around you, as it appears to be. As you think, so you create.* Our beliefs, values and conditioning start as soon as we are born into this world. During our early years as small children we take on the beliefs and conditioning from our parents. Added in to this whilst we are still children there is further conditioning from our society through the media, our peers and teachers.

The combination of the above together with our varied childhood experiences culminates in our beliefs regarding how we see the world and how it operates. This in turn results in how we think and how we react to different situations or people and helps create our desires for things. By the time we have reached adulthood we have firmly established beliefs and therefore have established how and what we think. *How you think is the worldly you.* It creates your personality and is how you perceive the world. It also manifests the world that you experience for yourself. Thoughts lead to more thoughts, lead to beliefs, lead to words, lead to actions. Your thoughts, beliefs, words and actions create the world as you experience it. Your personality or your worldly self is the result of a combination of your dominant thoughts.

The world as you experience it works as a reflection of your thoughts and beliefs. Your world therefore changes as your thinking changes. If you wish to change your world or the way you live your life, and wish to attract situations, objects, people or affluence then firstly consider the things that you are saying to yourself, the way that you think.

This world, your world, is a reflection of the inner you. Once you are able to change the inner you, the way that you think, the reflection of this thinking, the outer world or physical world, will automatically change.

Achieving Material Success through the Ego or Worldly Self

Most people who are currently materially very successful in our society have been fortunate in that their childhood conditioning and experiences resulted in them having very strong dominant thoughts about achieving material success. The reason they have been successful is that their dominant thoughts were of success and achievement, and they had these thoughts nearly all of the time. Most of their attention and therefore most of their thoughts were about how to be successful and this resulted in action.

Thinking leads to outcome

Much thinking about success leads to material success

This is how the vast majority of successful people have achieved their success. This is, as was referred to earlier in this book, the currently accepted way to achieve success. It is achieved firstly through past conditioning in childhood leading to strong thoughts and therefore a strong belief in being successful. Success sooner or later appears.

There is however a high price to pay. Success is achieved mainly through the ego or thinking mind, with large payments of anxiety, worry, fear, broken relationships, conflict, inner unhappiness and unrest. Success has been attained at the price of happiness. This is ironic, as of course if you ask people why they want to be successful, the eventual answer is always 'to be happy'.

We can therefore ask whether the secret of happiness is *not* to be successful and *not* to wish for success? This is not necessarily so, as most people who have not attained a high level of success or even who are not materially successful at all, also do not experience true happiness. They too regularly fluctuate between happiness and unhappiness characterized by unease, worry, anxiety, restlessness, boredom or worse.

The reason that many, both materially successful and non-successful people feel unease and discontentment is because they totally identify with the ego or the worldly self all or most of the time. For most people the consciousness of *I am*, the observer, the true or higher self is fully entwined with their thoughts, objects, their ego and with other people. *The way to inner peace and true happiness is to wake up from the dream of thought, from sleepwalking through life and to realize that we are both the observer, and watcher of thoughts as well as being the thinker of thoughts.*

Once we realize that our higher self is the observer of the thinker or the observer of our thoughts, the consciousness *I am* starts to become disentwined from our thoughts, disentwined from our ego or our worldly self and we start to experience the true power of happiness along with the power to manifest the life we desire in a non-attached easy and happy way.

How to Bring the Consciousness of your True Self into your World and Start to Experience True Happiness

You can start to experience true happiness by creating space between your thoughts. The gateway is the present moment, when you are able to let go of thoughts. When you live from the present moment of no thought you will find that people, situations and circumstances that you would like to appear in your life will gradually come to you with ease.

You will come to experience true happiness and success, without sacrifice, force, desperation or insecurity. You will have woken up to life, woken up from the dream of thought, to experience your eternal self beyond thought and you are then able to truly enjoy your worldly life here and now.

In order to experience true happiness you firstly need to be able to let go of thoughts and to start experiencing a space between thoughts. As you learn to temporarily let go of thoughts you begin to align yourself with your higher self which has perfect knowledge, perfect intelligence, perfect creativity, perfect joy, perfect love and perfect peace.

Before we go on to explore exercises and techniques which help you temporarily stop thinking when you wish to thereby creating a space between thoughts, it will be helpful to firstly explore the truth of universal consciousness and the spiritual secret of manifesting.

Chapter 4

The Spiritual Secret of Manifesting – Experience Your Divine Essence

The world we live in and the physical universe itself exists in the manifest realm, or to put it another way in the physical realm. The source of all creation, everything in the physical world is the unmanifest realm. It is the source out of which the earth, the physical universe, our bodies, plants, animals and all physical objects have manifested or come into being.

The manifest realm is the realm we all know and can perceive through our various senses of sight, hearing smell and touch. The unmanifest realm is the realm we cannot see and cannot perceive through our senses. It is invisible and unknown to our senses. Other words for the unmanifest are the universal self, universal intelligence, universal consciousness, universal spirit or divinity. The unmanifest expresses itself through the manifest or physical world. The life force which is within all humans, all living creatures and nature is that of universal consciousness or divine essence.

Universal consciousness has given life to the manifested universe, including human beings, nature and all living creatures in this world. Furthermore universal consciousness is also within the whole physical universe. It is both the consciousness that gives life to everything in the physical universe, including the sun, the stars, the earth, plants, animals and human beings and is the life force within. As universal consciousness or divinity is the life force within all living things and the whole of nature, it experiences the interaction of forms with each other, and therefore experiences itself through these interactions of the numerous forms in the manifest world.

However our senses, including our thinking mind, can only experience physical forms. Our senses are unable to experience and know the unknown, the invisible, the unmanifest, the universal consciousness of which our true selves are part of. This is why the vast majority of people, especially in the western world, are unable to experience the universal consciousness or divine essence within themselves and all around themselves.

In order to experience it we need to have our attention away from thinking, as thinking itself is a form. It is an energy form and as an energy form it also exists in the manifest. The more we are thinking the more we are in our ego and the less the connection we experience to the universal intelligence or consciousness that is within us and all around us. *The more we are able to stop thinking when we choose to, the more we are able to connect to our higher self, the part of universal consciousness or life force that is within us.* Through our higher, non-thinking self we can then connect to the whole of the universal consciousness or intelligence which is present in the whole of the physical universe.

Neither our senses nor our thoughts can experience universal consciousness or the divine. The reason for this is that for most people all or most of their attention is outwards into the physical world. All their attention is directed outwards towards objects, situations and people in this world or else their attention is on their thoughts which are energy forms about objects, situations or people in this world.

In order to experience the divine essence, or higher self within, we need to start taking our undivided attention away from the physical objects of this world and also away from thinking. In doing this we are taking our attention away from the manifest realm and towards the unmanifest.

At the level of our higher self everything in the universe is connected. Furthermore at the level of our higher self, which is part of universal consciousness, everything is in unity. The universal consciousness which gives life is within all human beings, creatures and nature. *At the level of our higher self we are therefore connected with the rest of the universe and subsequently when we access and experience our higher self or divine essence, which is a part of universal consciousness that is within us, we are able to have a real influence on the world we live in*. We can then change our circumstances in this physical world in which we are living by firstly having an intention for something, someone or circumstances to appear in our world. *Intention is a desire but without attachment to the result*. Once we start to access and experience our higher self, the physical world as we experience it will start to change. *The universe itself will be on our side and will start making slight rearrangements for our intentions to manifest.*

The more we are able to feel and maintain a connection and experience our higher self, the more we become the observer as well as the observed. We become to know and experience ourselves as the observer of our thoughts and when *you* start to do so *your* life will begin to change for the better.

Life will become easier, you will be luckier, helpful coincidences will happen, people will be drawn to you and the things you wish for in your life will start to appear. The time it takes to manifest the life and things you desire will be dependent on the degree to which the connection to your higher self is maintained, whilst you go about your destiny of creating the life you desire. For some people the life they wish to manifest appears quickly and for others the changes happen more gradually.

The alternative, which is what the vast majority of our society is presently doing, is to create their lives only through the ego or thinking mind, which is creating through past conditioning, attachments and fears. All negative emotions and negative thoughts are various aspects of fear. These include amongst others worry, anxiety, anger, violence, restlessness, jealousy, nervousness, hate, manipulation, defensiveness and force. Whatever people create through the ego will only bring a short period of satisfaction or pleasure. The process of creativity through the ego goes hand in hand with unhappiness. Fleeting pleasure if people get what they want and pain if they do not.

This is not how it has to be. *There is another way for us all to live and create in the world.* The secret of life here on earth is to realize and experience our higher eternal self. The more we experience our higher self the more happiness we will directly feel and experience, and therefore the more we will create our life through happiness and the more happiness we will bring to people around us.

The Secret of Life

Throughout the ages people have always wondered and asked themselves "What is the secret of life and why are we here?" I believe the answer is twofold.

Firstly – To realize and experience our higher self, which is to awaken from believing we are just our ego, or a combination of our thoughts. To realize we are both the observer as well as the observed.

Secondly – To subsequently create our lives out of the resulting happiness and not out of the fears and attachments of the ego. When we create out of the feeling of happiness life becomes easy. We are able to create through effortless action so that objects, situations, people and affluence will be attracted into our lives if we so desire.

We will then start to see everything and everyone afresh and feel more of a connection with people, animals and nature. We will directly feel more peace, joy and happiness. Life starts feeling magical.

The following verse is from the *Tao Te Ching*, a book of ancient teachings from the time of Confucius around 500 B.C. which along with many other spiritual teachings from around the world have pointed towards the universal consciousness or divinity that is within us and all around us.

> *"A mind free of thought*
> *Merged within itself*
> *Beholds the essence of Tao*
> *A mind filled with thought*
> *Identified with its own perception*
> *Beholds the mere forms of this world"*

Tao has been translated as the *supreme reality*. The supreme reality is universal consciousness or in other words divinity.

Chapter 5

How to Access the Power of Manifesting

The gateway for accessing the power to manifest is the present moment of no thought. The following actions and meditations can be used to help to create space between thoughts and to experience the first glimpse of your higher self, which can only be experienced when the mind is quiet.

Solitude and Silence

A good starting point is to allocate some time each day for you to be alone. Give yourself permission to have thirty minutes or more to yourself. Start by sitting in a comfortable chair and just relax. You will probably have thoughts occurring to you, however realize that you do not have to hold on to the thoughts and just let them go. Consider thoughts as passing driftwood that you can allow to just float away. Once you realize you can just let them pass, they will appear and then pass away. If another thought comes allow yourself to let that go as well and it will quickly pass. After a week or so practicing this exercise of solitude and silence you will feel your mind starting to quieten during these periods and you will start to experience space between thoughts, a period of no thought, which you will find to be a very peaceful place.

Breathing Meditation

In order to help you extend the period of no thought, concentrate on your breathing. This works by taking your attention away from the mind and in to the life energy within your body. As you take your attention away from the mind the mind starts to become still. The easiest way to do this is simply by sitting in a chair in silence and solitude somewhere in your house or garden, where there is no television or music in the background, and just concentrate on your breathing.
During all meditations you should not be driving or operating machinery.

Begin by closing your eyes, sitting upright and relaxed and take a deep breath, *breathing from your stomach* and filling your lungs. At the end of the inward breath hold the breath for a couple of seconds then slowly let it out. When you have fully exhaled *pause* for three seconds or so before inhaling once again.

Throughout the breathing have your attention

fully on your breath. Have your attention on your breath as you fully breathe in following your breath as it moves into and fills your lungs. Keep your attention on the breath as you hold it for a couple of seconds and then as you then slowly breathe out. Finally keep your attention on the area inside of your body, behind your heart area for three seconds or so, prior to breathing in once more.

As you practice this breathing technique more and more you will find yourself going deeper and deeper into a place of relaxation and your mind will begin to stop having thoughts during this time. You will have started to experience the happiness and peace of no thought. You will have started to connect to your eternal higher self, and through your higher self you have a connection with the whole of universal consciousness.

When you are ready to finish your breathing session just take your attention away from your breathing and become fully aware of the room around you. Once you have practiced it a few times you should experience an extended period of no thought throughout the meditation.

Relaxation Meditation

Begin by sitting in a comfortable chair in a quiet area of the house and close your eyes. This meditation, as others, is designed to take your attention away from your thoughts and into your inner body. Start by putting your attention on your left foot and say to yourself "Relax your left foot". Keep your attention on your left foot for another five seconds or so. Then move your attention to your right foot and say to yourself "Relax your right foot". Keep your attention on your right foot for approximately five seconds. You then continue on through the different parts of your body in the same way. After the left foot then the right foot progress in the natural order from your feet up to your head. Left calf, left thigh, right calf, right thigh, left hand, left forearm, left upper arm, right hand, right forearm, right upper arm, left buttock, right buttock, lower back upper back, stomach, chest, left shoulder, right shoulder, neck, left cheek, right cheek, chin, jaw, left ear, right ear, back of head, forehead and finally eyes. The order of relaxation can vary, but should start at the feet and move upwards. Once you have relaxed the various areas of your body say to yourself "Relax your whole body".

This meditation will help to quieten your

mind the very first time you do it. Your body will feel relaxed, your mind will be quietened and you will start to experience a feeling of peace. The more often you practice this relaxation meditation the more relaxed you will feel and the more peace you will feel.

Once you have relaxed your eyes just stay with the feeling you experience for five minutes or so to begin with, which you can then extend if you wish to each time you meditate. As with the previous exercise when you are ready to finish the meditation just take your attention away from your body, open your eyes and become fully aware of the room around you.

Self Observation with Your Eyes Closed

Be the observer of your thoughts. Start by sitting comfortably in a quiet room with your eyes closed. As we have established earlier you are not just a combination of your thoughts, your worldly self, but also the observer of your thoughts, your higher self. You are the observer *and* the observed. This exercise therefore will help you to create space around your thoughts and will help you to take attention away from your thoughts as they occur, when you wish to do so. As thoughts appear just observe them, do not judge them, and just observe in a detached manner, keeping as much attention as possible on your inner body, on the life force within you.

Self Observation with Your Eyes Open

Try keeping your attention on the observer or your higher self whilst your eyes are open and as you look around the room or outside at nature. As you look around you may find yourself labeling objects that you see. Most people are unable to simply look at an object without labeling it, without the mind commenting. Most people when looking at a chair will say to themselves "chair", or when looking at a table they will say "table" to themselves. To be precise their mind will say "table". This tends to be the same for all objects including those things in nature such as trees, mountains and clouds and also when looking at other individuals.

If our minds are constantly labeling and comm.-enting as we look at objects, nature and other people our minds are not still and we are merely able to experience the forms that we are looking at. However once we are able to quieten our minds and to observe objects, other people and nature whilst maintaining our attention more within ourselves, more in our higher selves we are able to feel and experience more than merely the form. We are able to experience the life energy within forms, the essence of universal consciousness within other forms, and therefore we are able to feel the real connection and unity with everything and everyone.

An Exercise in Being the Observer

Following meditation, open your eyes and keep your attention within your body whilst observing the clouds in the sky or a tree in your garden. *Do not label or comment on the clouds or the tree* just observe. If your mind is quiet you will find an extra quality to the clouds or the tree that you may never have experienced before. Their true beauty will be revealed to you.

You can also do this same exercise with your pets, your partner and later with strangers. Your connection with nature, animals and others will be significantly increased. You will be experiencing things beyond mere form. You will be experiencing the same divine essence in nature, animals and other people that is within yourself. The result is a feeling of oneness with everything in this world.

Manifesting Happiness – Full method

- *Practice silence and solitude for five minutes*

- *With your eyes closed relax all parts of your body with your attention on each part as you relax them. At the end say "relax your whole body"*

- *Put attention on your breathing to begin with and then start taking your attention away from the breathing and in to your body around the heart area. You should then be aware of your breathing but also feel detached from it, with most of your attention/consciousness within your body.*

Each step brings you an increasing feeling of peace and joy. The more times you practice this technique the more connection you will feel to your higher self beyond thought. This is the place of manifesting consciousness or true happiness which I have called manifesting happiness. When you are at this point you will want to stay there for a while. When you open your eyes, this feeling of peace and joy will stay with you for a while. Whenever it starts to wane you may choose to repeat the meditation. Meditate twice a day if possible, first thing in the morning and last thing at night.

After you have followed the main practice a number of times you should be able to reach the place of peace by following the quick method below. The quick method can be used to help keep you centered to your true self and you will therefore experience a feeling of background peace, happiness and contentment.

Manifesting Happiness – Quick method

- *Say to yourself "Relax your whole body". Begin by putting your attention on your breathing and then put more and more of your attention within your body around the heart area whilst still observing your breathing.*

The exercises and meditations that have been outlined in this chapter are designed to create space between and around your thoughts, to give you a glimpse of your higher self. As you do these exercises regularly in the comfort of your own home you will also find that in your day-to-day life as you go about your tasks you will have longer periods of no thought and be more in the present moment. You will still find yourself thinking about the past and the future but increasingly you will be aware of this and by becoming aware you will bring yourself back to the present moment. Look out for feelings of unease, restlessness, worry or discontent in order to realize that you have taken your attention away from the present moment of no thought, and then bring your attention back to the present moment.

A few conscious breaths as described in the breathing exercises will help you to do so. To help let go of the past and future and to come back to the present moment also realize that your thoughts are often making you unhappy and decide to choose instead true happiness for yourself.

Later in the book I will explain further universal laws and secrets which will enable you to help choose when you think and what you think about. These truths will enable you to experience longer and longer periods of true happiness and contentment, and also greatly increase your power to manifest the things you desire.

Chapter 6

The Secret Spiritual Formula for Success

Inner Happiness + Clear Detached Intention + Present Moment Effortless Action = That Which You Desire = Success

The 4 Steps

To be able to manifest anything you want in your life follow the 4 steps.

1) Firstly experience happiness in the present moment by practicing extended periods of no thought. Once you are experiencing true happiness through extended periods of no thought you are then able to start creating or manifesting out of happiness.

2) Secondly have a clear intention of that which you wish for to be attracted in to your life. This needs to be done in a detached way, which means that you do *not* desperately want or need it to happen in order for you to be happy some time in the future.

3) Thirdly put your attention in the present, by putting your attention on the actions you

need to take now in order to help your intention to manifest. If you are unsure what actions to take in the present, go in to a period of no thought, and soon you will know what to do.

4) Take present moment effortless action.

Inner Happiness + Clear Detached Intention + Present Moment Effortless Action = the Manifesting of Your Desires

The Practical Process

Firstly consider the life you wish to live. In order to have a clear picture of this life it is helpful to consider the following:

- The people you wish to be mostly around in your life. These may be your partner, family, friends and your work colleagues. Consider the qualities of people you wish to spend most of your time with.
- Where you would like to live, the type of house and location.

- The type of work or business you would like to be involved in and which you would enjoy.
- The hobbies and pastimes you would like to enjoy.
- The way you would like to feel, for example a life where you enjoy good health and one in which you feel inner peace and enduring happiness.
- Your balance of time spent in different areas of your life. The percentage of time spent with your partner, pursuing hobbies, working, resting and vacationing.

After clearly considering and imagining your ideal happy and successful life, write this down in detail. Picture this ideal life that you wish to be living and then write down the elements of it. Next choose a time scale in which you wish this life to be manifested. This time scale should be the shortest that you could possibly imagine that any person in your current life situation in your society could achieve, if everything went right. Remember not to limit your desires, but to *be positive* and to *reach for the stars.* A five year time scale is generally one that works best, but if you have a stronger present belief then you may wish to choose a time scale of maybe three of four years. There are pages at the end of this chapter for you to write down your ideal life situation, together with your long-term or five year goals. Please see the following example. Your goals will of course vary from this example.

Within Five Years

- *I have the personal qualities of composure, courage, confidence, creativity, good communication and decisiveness. I am relaxed and happy.*
- *I enjoy a loving and happy life with a partner I love and who loves me.*
- *I drive a new Porsche 911 Carrera.*
- *I own a large five-bedroom house with an outdoor spa and beautiful views of countryside, hills and trees.*
- *I have a net worth of approximately two million dollars.*
- *I have plenty of free time and enjoy a balanced lifestyle of work, rest and play.*
- *I am fit and healthy, exercising two to three times a week and am truly happy.*
- *I enjoy spending time with family and friends.*

- *I enjoy extended sunshine vacations each year meeting new people.*
- *I work from home for a total of two to three days a week.*
- *I experience an enduring feeling of inner peace and inner happiness.*
- *I am happy and successful*

Next Set Your One Year Goals

These should be viewed as stepping stones, which move you towards your five year goals.

Within One Year

- *I have met a loving partner with whom I feel a real connection and with whom I have shared values and interests. Or if you already have a partner, I have a happy and loving relationship with my partner.*
- *I am running a successful business which I really enjoy.*
- *I have plenty of time for rest and relaxation.*

- *I join a tennis club and play tennis two to three times a week.*
- *I spend quality time with my family and friends.*
- *I eat and drink healthily.*
- *I am happy, healthy and successful.*

Next write down personal philosophies that will be helpful in realizing your happiness and success.

Personal Philosophies

- *I live in the present moment as much as possible with my full attention on that which I am doing at present.*
- *I meditate once or twice a day.*
- *I enjoy regular walks in the countryside or park.*
- *I give my partner, family and people I meet my full present moment attention.*
- *I forgive people when their actions do not match what I expected.*
- *I go with the flow of life and expect things to turn out well.*
- *I enjoy regular exercise.*
- *When talking with others I keep a friendly tone in my voice, even when I am discussing a problem or*

someone has not done what I asked of them.
- *I remember people usually reflect back to me how I am with them. I therefore have a warm regard for others at all times.*
- *I give first knowing in giving I am receiving;*
    - *To have friendship I am friendly towards others first.*
    - *To have love I give love to others first.*
    - *To have respect I give respect to others first.*
    - *To have harmony I am harmonious towards others first.*
    - *To receive money I provide a product or service which truly helps others.*
    - *To receive understanding I give understanding towards others first.*
    - *To be accepted I accept others first.*
    - *To receive help I am helpful towards others first.*
- *I eat and drink healthily realizing that what I eat and drink will affect the way I feel.*
- *I put my attention on the things I want to happen without putting too much attention on problems or perceived problems.*
- *I accept how things are at present without blaming anyone including myself. I then have an intention to change things if required.*

- *I realize that in all problems there are opportunities. I ask myself what is life telling me and how can I learn from this? What is the solution and the opportunity? I realize that things, at any given moment, are as they are meant to be. I accept and make friends with the present moment. If it is possible to change the situation I have a goal to do so and make a plan to do so, but importantly I do this in a detached way and without fighting the present moment as I realize that which I resist will persist.*
- *I remember that the enjoyment is in the journey not the destination, life always happens in the present moment.*
- *I realize that humor is great for feeling good and being in the present moment. I don't take myself or life too seriously, I have a laugh!*
- *I don't watch negative television programs or listen to or watch too many commercials.*

In order to manifest your goals/intentions more quickly, firstly read your five year goals slowly and out loud if possible, then immediately meditate for ten to fifteen minutes using the meditation techniques described earlier. Whilst in meditation there should be no thought. The purpose of meditating is to help you achieve a state of no thought and to make a connection with your higher self, the powerful self which is beyond thought and which is connected with everything else in the universe.

In order for something to be manifested into your life you introduce an intention or intentions/goals, for example your life's five year goals *prior* to meditation. Whilst you are in effective meditation there should be no thoughts whatsoever, however by slowly reading your goals which you wish to manifest, just prior to meditating, these thoughts will be present just before you go in to meditation and will therefore also be present immediately following meditation. Your higher self will pick these up. You will therefore start to have the cooperation of universal intelligence to create circumstances in which your goals manifest themselves.

Remember the secret spiritual formula for success:

Inner Happiness + Clear Detached Intention + Present Moment Effortless Action = the Life You Wish to Manifest = Success

The reading out loud of your five year goals is the *clear detached intention*, the connection to your higher self is the *true happiness. The effortless action* is the action that you decide to take in the present moment in order for your one and five year goals to manifest.

By *meditating once a day for the first two weeks on your five year goals/detached intentions,* the right effortless actions will come to you. However do not force this to happen, just stay happy and relaxed and in the present moment and the action or actions that need to be taken in the present moment will come to you. *After the first two weeks, meditate on your five year goals just once a month* in order that your goals *do not* become attachments and to enable you to concentrate on present moment action in order to fulfill these goals.

The purpose of your one year goals and your list of personal philosophies is to help you take effective present moment action in order to move you towards your five year goals. I would suggest that only the five year goals are read prior to meditating in the first two weeks in order that your higher self is clear as to what your real goals are. However after the first two weeks when you will be reading your five year goals only once a month prior to meditating it is recommended that you read your one year goals and personal philosophies immediately prior to daily meditation. The only exception to this is on the one day each month when you read and meditate on your five year goals.

Always make your goals positive, they are the goals that you want to happen not those that you do not want to happen. This is very important in that your attention is on *positives and not negatives.* The reason being that the things we put our attention on in our lives increase or appear and those things we take our attention away from tend to disappear, for example if you are saying I do not want to be ill, the 'do not' is not heard by the higher self and the intention is on illness. Instead the goal would be: *I enjoy good health.*

Your goals should be written in the present tense as though they were already happening or already manifested. For example, instead of I want or I wish, write such things as I have, I own or I am. For instance *I own a lovely five bedroom house on a large plot.*

Remember to include desires or goals in relation to the type of person you wish to be. For example, I have the qualities of courage, confidence, creativity, energy, communication, composure and decisiveness. I am successful in everything I do. I am relaxed and happy. I have self-motivation and motivate others.

Remember to set your goals or desires high enough. Do not put self-imposed limits to your desires. *It is also very important to write down your goals or desires when you have a feeling of happiness within.* You will then know more accurately what is good for you and what you truly want in your life. *A good way of doing this is to practice one or more of the meditation exercises outlined earlier, prior to the initial writing of your goals or desires.*

Do not think or worry about how the goals or desires will manifest as you write them down. Just experience the inner feeling of happiness and write down the goals or desires whilst maintaining a non-attachment to the desires themselves or how you will achieve them. Imagine you are writing a book or movie about your life with you as the main character. Imagine the way you wish your character, *you* to feel in your life and the life situations you wish your character *you* to experience.

The more you are able to have periods of no thought outside of your daily meditation time the quicker the effective present moment action needed will come to you and the easier it will be to carry out the action. Also the quicker your goals will come about.

When the best effective action to achieve your one year goals has come to you, remember to be in the present moment when carrying out the actions and have your full attention on these present moment actions. *The more attention you have on your current actions the better the quality of the action and the more effective the action will be.* The more effective your current actions are in the pursuit of your goals the quicker your goals and the life you desire will manifest.

Remember once you are aware of and practice the secret of true happiness revealed earlier you will find that you are happy in yourself right now. You will be living in the present moment, which is where the joy of life takes place and you will feel inner happiness. You will also know that your happiness does not depend on the external things of this world that are in constant flux.

We all have the power to create and manifest the circumstances of our lives and once we have found happiness within we are able to create and manifest our lives from a position of happiness and not from fear which will in turn benefit both ourselves and the people around us, and therefore society as a whole.

It is important to remember not to be too attached to your goals otherwise you will be creating out of fear and not out of happiness. If you create out of fear you will be unhappy now and still unhappy in yourself in the time after the goals have been met. However when you create out of happiness you will be happy both now and happy on the realizing of your dreams or goals. *You will enjoy the journey as well as the achievements. Remember the journey itself is what life is about, not the destination.*

My 5 Year Goals

&

Things I wish to manifest within 5 years

★ _____

★ _____

★ _____

★ _____

★ _____

★ _____

★ _____

★ _____

★ _____

★ _____

★ _____

★ _____

My 1 Year Goals

୬

Things I wish to manifest within 12 months

★ _____

★ _____

★ _____

★ _____

★ _____

★ _____

★ _____

★ _____

★ _____

★ _____

★ _____

★ _____

Personal Philosophies I wish to Practice Now

★ _____

★ _____

★ _____

★ _____

★ _____

★ _____

★ _____

★ _____

★ _____

★ _____

★ _____

★ _____

Chapter 7

The Secret Keys to Your Happiness and Success

Continued non-attachment to your intentions/goals is the key to you feeling present moment happiness and also the key for the detached intentions to manifest quickly. As you clearly want the various things, people and situations to appear in your life you will of course have a certain amount of attachment to these things. The key to your continued happiness and success and for these detached intentions to manifest quickly is to remain detached from them. *Please therefore do not make these intentions into attachments.*

The more attachment you have to your goals or desires the more you will find yourself thinking about them and therefore the less connection you will keep to your higher self, which is the true power which brings about real change in your life situation. The secret key is to keep your desires or intentions as detached desires and intentions.

Non-Attachment to Desires – The Secret Key

Universal intelligence wants you to be abundant in all things including happiness, love, success, health, freedom and also wealth. Universal intelligence wants you to succeed, it wants you to be happy, healthy and successful. It wants for you what you want for yourself. It wants you to enjoy the good things of this world including those things that money can buy. *Universal intelligence is on your side.*

Through your connection to your higher self, which is in turn part of universal intelligence, universal intelligence knows what your desires are and can start to change things so that these desires can be manifested into your life. However, attachments to desires loosen your connection to your higher self and therefore your connection to universal intelligence or universal consciousness. The reason for this is that the more attachment you have for something to happen, the more you think about it and the more you worry that it won't happen. Subsequently you are residing only in your ego or worldly self much more. The more this happens the less connection you maintain to your higher self.

Keeping Your Desires or Intentions Detached

- *Knowledge and belief that universal intelligence or divinity wants what you want, and is on your side. Following the reading and meditation on your goals, let them go allowing universal intelligence to take care of them.*

- *Live in the happiness of uncertainty staying detached from thoughts about your goals.*
- *Maintain the quality of patience – allow the goals or detached desires to come about when the time is right.*
- *If you find yourself thinking or worrying too much about your goals or desires instead choose happiness now rather than suffering through too much thinking and attachment.*

The Spiritual Secret of Living in the Happiness of Uncertainty

Nearly everyone wants to feel in control of their lives and therefore they feel a need to control both other people and life situations. Because people wish to feel in control of their life they also tend to worry about the future. They may worry about a number of things that may or may not happen in the future along with worrying about how they could deal with problem situations if they did happen.

Often the reason people wish to be in control is because of fear, fear that they will not be secure. This may relate to financial security, relationship security and health security amongst other things. People feel insecure about money, relationships, health and other things and they think they will feel more secure if they can control situations and people, to force things to happen as it suits them. This can work for a time, although it can take a lot of energy and also causes unease, anxiety and unhappiness when an individual constantly tries to control other people and situations through forcefulness.

Eventually relationships and success which have been acquired or maintained by control and force tend to disappear, to fall apart. Even if they do not, the individual that is the controller is unhappy as the constant requirement to maintain and control a situation or relationship through force or forceful behavior takes its toll, resulting in anxiety, worry and health problems.

Life on earth is in constant flux, and from the position of the ego self it is very difficult to control. Things are always changing, problems always occurring, people always doing what they *shouldn't do*. And we feel as though we need to control everything, to control life. Because of this we feel the need to be continually on guard, ready to attack as necessary, ready to use force to get our way and to always be wary. Therefore we feel a constant need to be looking forward to see what could go wrong so that we can try to make plans now to control things in the future. In doing this we hope to prevent things going wrong. But by living this way we are living and creating out of fear. It is clear that by trying to control life we will create much unhappiness for ourselves and we will be limited in how effective we can be.

Why do many people try to control life?

The answer is because of uncertainty. People are uncertain of the future, uncertain what will happen in the future. They therefore worry about all the things that potentially *may* happen which results in unhappiness in the present. People display controlling behavior in order to *force* things to happen or work out as they wish them to.

In their minds they are delaying their happiness for some time in the future when they think everything will be okay, everything will be certain, a time when they think they will feel secure and happy. *But happiness does not happen in the future. It can only be felt in the present moment, tomorrow never comes.*

A person who feels insecure and says to themselves "Once I make a million I will feel secure, and then I will be happy" will still not feel happiness and peace inside when they have made a million. He or she will still feel insecure and unhappy inside and may then aim for ten million to give them the peace, happiness and security they are looking for.

Things and objects in the outside world *do not* make us feel any lasting happiness inside. They are false rainbows and if we rely on external things and situations in our world for us to be happy we will find ourselves continually searching.

The secret is to live in the Happiness of Uncertainty.

To live in the happiness of uncertainty means you do not worry about the future. You do not worry "What if this happens or what if that happens". You are happy to live your life now in the present moment, to enjoy the journey, to enjoy your happiness in the present which you cannot do unless you are prepared to live in the happiness of uncertainty.

By living in the happiness of uncertainty you are saying to yourself the following;

- *Because life in this world is in constant flux, forever changing, I cannot know now exactly what the future will bring.*
- *When a decision or action is required I will have the knowledge at the time to take it, but I am not going to worry now about what may or may not*

> happen. I also know that my future is created in the present.
> - *The attention and therefore quality of my present moment actions and decisions is the key to the future. I know how I would like my life to be in one and five years time and have taken action in the present to draw up a plan of what to do now which will set me on my way for this to be realized.*
> - *I do not know the exact series of events that will transpire for me to reach my five year goals however I do know that the universe is on my side because I am not fighting against it.*

By having a goal or intention for the type of life situation you wish to be living and to then start living in the happy flow of life now, in the happiness of uncertainty, things will work out for you. The universal intelligence will help organize this, as you will be acting in harmony with it. As you live in the flow of life and in the happiness of uncertainty you have more attention in the present and are more able to see the best decisions and actions to take as well as seeing opportunities more clearly as they appear.

You do not force or control people or situations to be as you wish them to be. You realize that the present is as it is meant to be and that there is a better and more effective way of looking and dealing with situations that may appear to be problems to you. This results in a decision or course of action which will be right for you and those affected by your decision. The solution will therefore need no force to implement as it will be acceptable to everyone that is affected by it.

Abundant Patience

When you decide you want something to appear in your life you may also find yourself saying that you want it *now* instead of knowing that it will appear when the time is right. Therefore abundant patience is required in the sure knowledge that it will come about when the time is right.

Your ego or worldly self may try to question your spiritual approach to this, and start you thinking that your desires are not coming about quickly enough. It may start whispering to you to hand over control, in the guise of constant thinking and worrying, back to the ego or worldly self.

The key is to have abundant patience and to *know for sure* that the universe is on your side and that your intentions *will* come about when the time is right for you. The more patience you have the more you are able to live in the happiness of uncertainty and the more you are able to keep a connection to your higher self whilst taking present moment action for your detached desires to appear in your life.

Choose Happiness Now!

In addition to the above keys for remaining non-attached to the things you desire, you can also when required, just *choose happiness now*. If and when you are tempted to think and therefore worry about things that you wish to happen, instead say to yourself, *I know that if I start thinking about this now I will start feeling unhappy. If I can take some effective present moment action I will do so otherwise I choose to be happy now and will let these thoughts go.*

You now have the full framework needed to *experience happiness right now* and also for you to manifest or create that which your heart desires, whether it be success in obtaining money and material things, success in relationships, success in experiencing good health, or success in sport and hobbies.

The key to manifesting success is to live in the present moment, feeling a connection with your higher self, which results in you;

- Being happy and at peace now, in the present
- Taking effective action in the present moment that will attract your desires into your life
- Initiating the spiritual law of coincidence and good luck, whereby people, situations and even money and objects just appear in your life. Life becomes helpful to you.

I will expand on the spiritual law of good luck and coincidence in Chapter 10. In the following chapter we will explore the spiritual secrets for every day living which are practical ways for you to stay present and connected to your higher self when coming across challenging people and situations in your daily life.

Chapter 8

༄

Harmony in Everyday Living

Spiritual Secrets of Happiness, Influence and Attraction in Everyday Living

Everyday life and the situations and interactions in everyday life can sometimes pull us away from our connection to our higher selves and into our thinking mind/ego resulting in us feeling separated and unhappy.

There are many life situations that seem to pull us from our connection to our higher self and into the ego, some have a bigger pull than others. We all know people who are very much in their ego resulting in them acting in a dominant, argumentative or even aggressive way or just giving off bad vibes. These people can and even wish to pull you into their unhappy world and pull you into your own ego.

More accurately speaking people living very much in their ego can see other egos as a threat, and it is their ego which tries to pull you into the unhappiness they are feeling. The more that people live life from the viewpoint of their ego the more separated they feel from others and their higher self and therefore the more fearful and unhappy they generally feel. The resulting action depends on how strong their ego is and how much they are in their ego. If a person has a strong ego they will deal with the strong separation and fear they feel by judging, dominating or attacking others through thoughts, words or actions. Their thoughts result in them giving off bad vibes, their words can result in an aggressive, dominant or negative way of speaking and their actions can be the same through aggressive or negative looks, aggressive gestures and even violence or threat of violence towards another.

The dominant, aggressive or negative thoughts, words and actions from strong egos are designed to connect with your ego. This can produce reactions in your own ego. With many people this reaction is not difficult as they are also in their ego to a greater or lesser extent. When two equally strong egos meet each other the results can be strong disharmony, disagreement and even violence. This is because the more someone is in their ego the more separate, fearful and unhappy they feel, the more violence they feel and the more they feel they need to dominate others.

The Ego Self

The ego self, at a deep level, is very unsure of itself. It is fearful and negative and at times, in order to be surer of itself and to try and convince itself of its reality, it feels the need to attack others in some form or other. The individual ego self is a combination of thought and emotion and as such it is unstable, as both thoughts and emotions are in constant flux.

The more a person is identified with their ego self the more their thoughts and emotions are constantly changing. Subsequently the ego self experiences a regular need to feel real and unique and separate from others in order to feel that it exists. The ego self cannot get this from constant harmony with life and other people and therefore it often creates disharmony or drama in order to feel that it exists. This is experienced in a number of ways such as;

- Complaining about others or constantly complaining about situations, through thoughts, words or actions
- Judging others to be enemies
- Starting arguments
- Being moody
- Feeling bored
- Hostility or negativity towards others in thoughts, words or even actions
- Feeling or wanting to feel superior or better than others
- Demanding attention from others

You may come across this behavior from others in your personal relationships, at work or in your everyday life. In this chapter you will learn of the spiritual secrets which allow you to be mainly unaffected by the negativity of others, and also how to positively influence the behavior and actions of others.

The secret of happiness has already been shown to be experienced by substantially living in the present moment and therefore keeping a connection to your higher self. To do this we have established we need to be able to;

- Choose *not* to continuously think about things and people.
- Put our attention on the positives, when we choose to think. To put our attention on what we want to happen in our lives not that which we do not want to happen.
- Not be too attached to people, situations or objects otherwise they will be given too much power to make us suffer.
- Keep some of our attention within us, thereby remaining connected to our life energy or higher self, and not to have all our attention directed outward into the material world.

Of course if we were monks living in a secluded monastery it would probably be much easier to stay centered, to live in the present moment and therefore experience a feeling of happiness throughout our lives. One reason for this is that we would not tend to come across other people who are very much in their ego including work colleagues, our partner and family together with everyone we meet as we go through our daily lives. Also if we were in a monastery we would not need to earn a living in order to support ourselves and our family.

Within this chapter you will discover universal secrets for *everyday living* that are helpful in keeping you centered, present and happy so that life will feel easy. By practicing these truths you will experience an increased level of harmony within yourself and also with others, which will help you to enjoy harmony in your relationships both at work and at home. These secrets will result in you being able to influence the positive behavior of others. You will find that people are more attracted to you and are generally more helpful.

More Harmony and Happiness in your Encounters

We can all choose how we react to actions and words from other people and also how we react to life's situations and challenges as they arrive. If we encounter people who appear negative, argumentative or aggressive we firstly need to *forgive* them. People give off negative vibes, talk negatively and act negatively because at the time they are unhappy or fearful. Once you are aware of this it is easier to forgive people who are acting this way. Once you have forgiven them it is much easier *not to react to their negativity*. If someone says something negative to you, you do not need to react negatively back. By having some of your attention within yourself, on your higher self, you can remain detached from the situation and not be pulled in to it. This is because by having part of your attention within, you are acting as the observer as well as the observed and therefore you have space around the situation.

As such you do not react back in an automatic conditioned way but stay calm. You are then able to choose the best way to handle the person or situation in a detached way. By staying calm and detached the other person will be able to sense this and their negativity will start to ebb away. The calmness in your voice when you reply will be picked up by the other person, which in turn will not inflame the situation but will help to calm it down.

So as you come across negative people in your life, or more accurately people who are feeling unhappy within themselves which is manifested as negativity, your happiness will not be affected. In fact by remaining centered with part of your attention within, you are able to handle all situations that you encounter much easier and more effectively. Those people who act negatively will not be able to easily pull you into their unhappy world.

By not reacting like for like, you will encourage harmony both for yourself and for those people that you encounter. Remember to;

- Stay as the observer as well as the observed.
- Practice forgiveness.
- Practice non-reaction to people and situations.

By practicing this you will find that you have more harmony in your life. You will have more harmony in your relationships, your family life and at work.

By following the three steps above you will allow yourself to remain detached and centered and the most effective action or reply will come to you. The reply you give will be a non-reactive, non-conditioned reply. It will not be reactive and aggressive and will not therefore inflame any situation but help to create harmony.

This does not mean that sometimes the right reply or action may be to say that what someone is saying or doing is unacceptable, if that is what you feel. However when you reply you will be replying from a positive position of non-attachment and space, so the words will *not* be attacking, but said in a neutral tone which will also be much more effective and powerful than reacting in an angry, reactive tone.

Spiritual Secrets for Everyday Living

These truths are very practical ways for helping you to experience more happiness as you go about your daily life. By practicing these truths you will also find that people seem to be very helpful towards you and the goals and desires that you have previously written down and meditated on will start to come about with relative ease.

Secret 1 – Giving and Receiving

The easiest, most effective and quickest way to receive that which you desire is to give it first. As you give so you will receive. The key is to *give first*.

To receive more love, from your partner, family and friends *firstly* be more loving to them, and this will be reciprocated. You might give love by saying 'I love you' and giving them a cuddle, or by giving them your full attention when they are speaking. You may also show more interest in the things they are interested in by asking questions about how they are getting on and giving your full attention when they answer.

You may show more love by doing things for people, maybe cooking a special meal or arranging a nice surprise, or by buying a small surprise gift or by giving a genuine compliment. You will feel more love towards your partner by sometimes just watching them in the present moment without judgment, just as you can watch a sunset or sunrise. You can also give love by thinking kind and loving thoughts towards another.

To receive respect from someone, show respect first. To receive more co-operation, be more co-operative towards the other person. To be more successful help others to get what they want. To have more friends, be the first to be friendly. Say hello to others first and show your friendliness.

In fact whatever it is that you wish to appear more in your life, be prepared to be the first to show and give it toward *others. As long as the giving is genuine and with an open heart* you are assured to receive that which you have firstly given.

Secret 2 – Non-Judgment

Many people are constantly judging others and also constantly judging life's situations and events. They judge them to be good or bad rather than to accept people as they are, or to accept a life situation as it occurs. Judgment of people and situations is the ego commenting, which is what the ego can continually do. The key to non-judgment is forgiveness and full acceptance.

If we look back at our lives up until now we can often think of things that have happened which we judged to be bad at the time. However from the perspective of the present looking back and looking at the subsequent things that have come from a seemingly bad situation we can often now say that *it was for the best* that such a thing happened or did not happen at that time.

From the position of the ego or worldly self it is often very difficult to know at the time, when a situation you judge to be bad, is actually bad for you in the long term for your life happiness and success, or whether it turns out to be good in hindsight. People always say that *it is easy to see things with hindsight.*

Your higher self *can* see things in hindsight as they are occurring and therefore it knows what is good and what is bad for your happiness and success. It is therefore always trying to show you which decisions or actions to take. It does this through *intuition* or *gut feeling* and also by resistance to decisions you have already taken if the decision and action you have taken may not be in your best interests. The more you keep a connection to your higher self the more you will take decisions that are for the best. You will just know what to do.

When a problem or challenge occurs you will not force a solution on the problem as this can lead to more resistance or further problems. Instead, after re-looking at what you are doing or wanting to achieve you may see things slightly differently. You may realize that this is not the way forward or a different solution that does not include force may come to you.

You will also find that in every problem there is an opportunity. For every perceived problem look for the opportunity and you will find one, an opportunity for revealing more happiness and more success in your life.

Secret 3 – Forgiveness and Acceptance

People will not always act, say or do as we would wish them to and situations or life circumstances do not always happen as we would like them to. By firstly forgiving the person or circumstance that occurs we are more easily able to accept the situation as it is now. By forgiving we are then able to fully accept that which has occurred and therefore we do not suffer. We understand things are as they are at present. *We do not therefore fight against what is and make ourselves unhappy.*

In fact the more we do not fully accept things as they are at this moment of time the more we will resist them in our thoughts. The more we resist them the more we think about that which we see as undesirable and the more it is likely to persist.

Whatever is resisted will persist. By fully accepting what is at present we do not continue to fight against it and think about it continuously, which leads to the so-called problem continuing to make us feel unhappy. Once you have forgiven and accepted people or situations as they are at present you are accepting life as it is, you are making friends with life and life will be helpful towards you.

Forgiveness leads to acceptance, which leads to non-reaction. By forgiving a life situation that is undesirable to you, you are then able to accept it and this creates space around the situation which enables you *not* to react automatically to an undesirable situation occurrence or person. By automatically reacting to a negative situation or person you would be reacting out of the ego out of fear and conditioning which is likely to be unhelpful with regard to the situation or more usually would make it worse.

Forgiveness and acceptance creates space around your present life situation that also allows you to take *effective action*. You can more easily take effective decisions and actions depending on the situation and circumstances. Firstly you accept the situation so that it does not create further suffering for you. You are then able to respond to the situation with a creative solution that is not born out of automatic ego reaction and does not create further problems, as is almost always the case when an automatic ego reaction and subsequent action takes place with regard to difficult life situations or difficult people.

By accepting life situations, you will start to realize that most problems also bring with them opportunities. Opportunities to learn and change, to do something in a different and better way. If we are able to forgive and accept we are then more able to take effective action. Effective action can be defined as one that both benefits us and also benefits those people who are affected by the action. At the same time it is one that does not create further problems at a later date. It is non-ego based action. You will know the action to take when you need to know. When a decision has to be taken you will know what to do at that time, as you will be thinking clearly having maintained space around the problem by staying detached from the situation. The solution for other life situations that do not require immediate action will come to you in a similar way.

As a situation occurs you forgive the situation or person, including forgiveness of yourself if you think you have brought that situation about. This leads to acceptance of it that forgiveness enables. You maintain space around the situation by remaining detached. You are then able, at the time if required, or at a later time if not, to have a creative solution for dealing with it and to take effective action if action is required.

Secret 4 – The Easy Life

Most people wish to feel in control of their lives. They wish to control life to make it adhere to how they want it to be. As a result they always seem to find themselves fighting against life in order to make life be as they wish it to be. And in order to do this they find themselves fighting against other people who do not appear to be co-operating in this. There always seems to be problems to sort out, whether they are problem situations or problem people. Often people find themselves talking in an aggressive and demanding manner to others to try and force them to do what they want them to do, and therefore they will come across resistance.

As they see it the solution is to apply more force, more dominance, more attack until the ego of the other gives in to their will. This is how many people believe to be the best way to control their lives and to get what they want. Their actions come from the ego and they create and control their life from a position of fear. The result is unhappiness, unrest and anxiety for them and the same for people that resist them or get in their way. They use up a tremendous amount of life energy in order to control things that can leave them drained and exhausted over time.

The easy way is to live in the flow of life, to be more connected to your higher self and as a result to be more connected to everyone and everything else. You will then be able to create the life you wish for out of a position of happiness and not fear. You will then find that life appears easy and goes much more *smoothly*. You are not fighting against life but flowing with it. You will find yourself living life in a much less confrontational way, being much less confrontational towards others and therefore them towards you.

Your goal of course remains the same and that is to create a life that you wish for, and for that life to be an easy one. The difference is that you will be creating your life out of a position of happiness and not from the ego or fear. When you make decisions you take into account how the decision will affect others as well as yourself, therefore the decisions and actions you take are much more effective because you tend to have the support of others and the support of the universal intelligence or life itself. You enjoy the support because when you create your life from a position of happiness you are aligned with universal intelligence and the actions required to realize your goals are in alignment with it.

Also because you feel a greater connection to others you feel much more empathy towards them and they can sense this either consciously or unconsciously and will respond accordingly in a helpful manner. As you are in alignment with life itself, or universal intelligence which orchestrates everything, helpful coincidences will occur more and more often and *good luck will increasingly come your way*.

Situations which may appear to be problems will still happen but these will not daunt you as you realize that *things are as they are*, as *they are meant to be*. By forgiving the situation and accepting it you are able to remain more detached from it. The more challenging a problem may appear to be, the more you stay centered and calm and do not act in a reactionary or fearful way. Having fully accepted the situation you are able to take effective action by listening to your higher self.

Also as you have maintained a connection to your higher self, which is part of the universal intelligence, you will start to see the full truths of how things really are and how things work in our society. You can more clearly see the true motivations and therefore likely behavior of people you come across in both your personal and business lives. You are able to put yourself in their position and therefore know why a problem or situation has likely occurred. Once you understand that, it is easy to come up with effective action that will remedy the situation.

You will not force a solution on a problem but have a creative answer that does not include force or conflict, but takes into account the motivations, interests and goals or fears of everyone affected by the decision. A decision is then taken that is primarily of benefit to you but importantly it is also the best decision overall for everyone affected by that decision.

By practicing these four spiritual secrets in everyday life you will find life is easier and that people are more helpful towards you. You will start to experience a more harmonious life and your intentions and desires become far easier to manifest.

Chapter 9

The Start to a Great Day

Practical Ways to Manifest a Great Day for Yourself

We now know that what you say to yourself in your mental commentary will in time create who your worldly self is. *In this world, as you think, so you believe, so you act and so you are.*

You will tend to find that your day will unfold in the manner that relates to what you are thinking or saying to yourself after waking up in the morning, so it is important to start the day off with positive thoughts and positive intentions.

In this chapter you will read of practical ways to change any negative thoughts you have on waking to positive thoughts and intentions for the day ahead. If you wake up thinking and feeling negative about the day ahead this will probably be the kind of day you will have. The easy way to wake up with positive thoughts is to feel happy and positive prior to drifting off to sleep the previous evening. It is therefore helpful to do ten minutes of meditation in the evening so that you are feeling happy and positive *prior* to going to bed.

Gratitude and Happiness

At the start of the day or whenever you may be feeling slightly negative, a good way to instantly boost your mood and happiness is through the expression of gratitude. By expressing to yourself the gratitude you feel for all the good things in your life right now, you are putting your attention and therefore your energy on to the positives in your life.

As you consider those things in your life that you are thankful for, you start thinking about the good things in your life and your mood and happiness improves. *You cannot think about two things at exactly the same time;* therefore if you find yourself thinking about negative things you can turn this around by *expressing gratitude for the good things in your life. Your mind therefore starts transferring attention from the negative to the positive and you start feeling happier.*

You are feeling happier because you are thinking about good things and taking your attention and therefore energy away from negative or fearful things. You find that the things you put your attention on will increase in your life and conversely those that you take it away from will decrease.

Therefore through the expression of gratitude on a daily basis you feel happier and more of the good things that are present in your life will appear.

Mirror Technique

This is another practical technique that can help you boost the effectiveness of positive suggestion. It is a very simple and quick technique which simply involves looking at a reflection of yourself in the mirror whilst saying out loud the type of day you would like to have.

Firstly stand about a foot away from a mirror which is large enough for you to see your face and at least down to your chest. Allow any thoughts that you may have to disappear. If you are unable to do this then consider doing five minutes meditation first. This is not vital though as *the mirror technique works by distracting the mind.* The mind cannot think about negative and positive things at exactly the same time, it can only think about one thing, whatever that may be.

Stand in front of the mirror, standing tall and feeling powerful, and say out loud to yourself the three main things that you feel grateful for in your life. These three good things will help to put you in a positive frame of mind to begin with. Remain standing tall, shoulders back, relaxed and feeling powerful and look in the mirror into the reflection of your eyes. As you look deep into your eyes say out loud the type of day you are going to have and include your name as you talk. For example;

Andrew, you are so lucky to have good health, a loving partner and a lovely home which you share. You are going to have a great day today and things will go your way. You feel good, people are friendly and helpful and you will have achieved everything you want to easily and effortlessly.

Of course you can say anything positive to yourself that is relevant to the type of day you wish to experience, whilst you look right into your eyes in the mirror. Remember to include both how you wish to feel, as well as suggestions as to what you wish to achieve in the day.

The mirror technique can be practiced at any time when you wish to have a boost to your day, whenever you need to get the day back on course. It can be practiced at work before an important meeting or interview and also before a sporting event. The only difference is that you do not say the words out loud, for obvious reasons, if people are within hearing distance. But you would do it in the same way as described earlier, beginning by saying the three main things in your life that you feel gratitude for, which gets you feeling positive, and then look into your eyes and say to yourself how you wish the interview, meeting or sports event to go. As you are looking into your eyes you will start to get a good feeling and you will find that things will tend to go how you have wished them to.

Chapter 10

Messages from your True Self

Opportunities, Helpful Coincidences and Good Luck

Your higher self wants you to succeed. It is always looking out for you. Unlike the ego it truly wants you to be both happy and successful. It wants you to experience peace, happiness, love, freedom and all the beautiful things this world has to offer. Your higher self is connected to and part of the one universal self. It is connected to all things in this world and it knows the best decisions to make, the best actions to take and the best behavior for you at any given present moment in order for you to enjoy happiness and success. To achieve this your higher self constantly tries to send you messages or give you signs to let you know the best way forward, the best decisions and actions to take when needed. These messages can come in a number of ways.

Intuition

You receive a *gut feeling*, an intuition comes to you with regard to a path or decision to take, one that just feels right. It may be an answer or solution to a problem which is apparent, or it may be one that propels you forward towards your life goals. You do not follow it blindly but ask yourself, whilst remaining centered and non-attached, what would be the likely outcome of this decision? What are the upsides and downsides? If it still feels right follow your instinct.

Resistance to Decisions and Actions

It may be that you are planning on taking a decision to either do something, meet someone, go somewhere or buy something. As you go about putting the plans into action you may begin to meet resistance in the form of a difficulty of some type. You may be looking to buy a particular item and it seems very hard to find what you are looking for, or it may be that you are planning to meet with someone and you are finding it very difficult to arrange the meeting, or it may be that you are planning to go somewhere and you keep coming up against problems in the arrangements or perhaps you are planning something else which does not seem to be coming about easily.

Whenever you meet any significant resistance to your actions it is wise to re-look at your decision and subsequent action and to ask yourself "Is this what I really want to do? Is this the best thing for me and all those affected by this decision?" Whenever significant resistance to your actions occurs it is best not to force or control the situation, not to force your will on a situation for it to come about. This is the time to reconsider what you are doing and why you are doing it. It is also worth re-looking at the situation from other people's points of view that may be affected by your actions. Ask yourself,

- Is this really what I want to be doing?
- How will the decision affect others?

You may decide that *yes this is what I want* and a creative solution will come to you that does not include applying more force against the resistance which is occurring. Alternately you may decide, *No, now that I consider it further I don't want to do this or take this action as I no longer feel this is the best decision for my happiness.*

Good Luck and Coincidences

The more you are on the right path and the more you feel a connection to your higher self the more you will become *lucky* with helpful coincideences occurring. People, situations and even gifts that are of help to you will appear as you need them. Universal intelligence or life will orchestrate these *coincidences* for you.

One personal example of good luck was the receipt of an unsolicited letter from a legal firm taking a group action with regard to some slight road noise from a road near to an investment property I own. I contacted the firm to check they were legitimate, and then I signed the form they had sent me to be included in the group action and then forgot all about it. About ten months later I wondered what had happened with regard to the legal action but thought nothing more of it. About a week later I received a check through the post for £7,500/$12,000! A good luck gift from life!

Chapter 11

❧

A New Way of Living

There are essentially two ways of living. You can live and create only through the ego, attachments and fear or else live and create with a connection to the higher self, non-attachments and happiness.

Living and Creating through your Ego

Living only through the ego entails obsessive thinking about both those things you desire and those things you do not want to happen or that you *fear* happening. The thinking goes hand in hand with strong attachments to the objects of desire or objects of fear. Living through the ego also involves control and force to get what you want, to force things to be as you wish them to be. Living through the ego also includes defense and attack against other egos.

The Effects of Living through the Ego

- Constantly being depleted of life energy resulting in more weariness, fatigue and health problems. As little connection is maintained with your higher self, life energy is only replaced through sleep.

- Desires with attachments resulting in obsessive thinking. Without being able to choose when and what to think about other thoughts such as doubts and fears and different competing desires will pass frequently across the mind, thereby the energy or life force given to your primary desires is much less, and often not enough for the desires to materialize.
- As you do not feel connected to the universal self you feel a sense of separation, of not being connected to everyone and everything else. You feel a background feeling of unhappiness or unease except for during brief spells.
- An increased number of problems. The less connection you have to your higher self, the less co-operation you will receive from the universal intelligence as you are cut off from it. You will therefore tend to experience more problems in your life.
- You will have background fear as a near constant companion, fear of not getting what you want and fear of things happening that you do not want to happen.
- Thinking is obsessive; you rarely stop thinking in order to experience peace and joy within yourself.

- You create your life through thinking about your fears and desires, through worrying. You experience a life of worrying.
- A need to feel in control. A need to control life's situations and other people through force, attack and defense against other egos and life itself.
- If desires and goals are achieved through obsessive thinking and control, only temporary happiness is experienced followed by the usual feelings of worry, fear and emptiness.

Living and Creating your life in Happiness through a Connection with your Higher Self

Because you have a connection via your higher self, to the rest of the universe and everything in it, you have a much greater ability to create. You have part of your attention within your body on your life force or higher self and part in this world. You have a foot in both camps. The intention given by the worldly self is taken up by the higher self, which is connected to all things on a higher level to bring about the intention. The more you are aligned with your higher self the easier it is to attract the things you wish for into your life.

Ego_____I_____The Higher Self

The further towards the higher self you reside, the easier and quicker it is to intend and manifest or attract things into your life. It is the quality of your connection to your higher self that occurs at the point just before and after your intention that creates whether and how quickly the desire manifests. Some desires which are smaller and easier to manifest can and do come about just by introducing an intention just before meditation, followed by living your life with a connection to your inner or higher self with nothing more needed.

For other desires that are bigger changes, there also needs to be present moment attention that works alongside the initial intention. The attention equates to present moment action to take in order to work alongside the higher self in manifesting your desires. The quality of your present moment action along with the initial intention will give rise to your desires manifesting when the time is right for you.

Benefits

- Desires and intentions are manifested quicker and without suffering for yourself and others you come in contact with or who are affected by your decisions. You live and create from a position of happiness and not fear. You can create in abandonment and will not be too attached to the outcome.
- You create and live your life without force and great effort. You live in the flow of life and life appears much easier and more helpful.
- You are a lot *luckier* in life, things seem to go your way and people appear to be more helpful and less confrontational.
- You do not feel separate, but feel a real connection to others, to animals and to nature.
- You do *not* have a background feeling of unease and unhappiness but feel a background feeling of peace and contentment as you go about your daily life.
- You live your life both as the observer and the observed and experience you true self.
- You experience better general health and wellbeing.

- Your relationships with others improve as you feel more connection with your partner, friends, family and work colleagues.

Effects

You can create and live the life you desire whilst experiencing a background feeling of happiness, peace and love. Every one of us is currently at a position on the continuum shown below somewhere between living totally in the Ego and living totally in the true self.

Ego_____I_____True Self

The purpose of this book is to help you awaken and become aware of your true or higher self so that you may consistently choose to move further up the continuum. As you do so you will enjoy more happiness and abundance in whatever you choose to do or create. You will live an easier and happier life now, creating abundance and success easier, from a position of more happiness and less fear.

Creating your Life through Happiness and a Connection to Your Higher Self – A Summary

1. Extended periods of no thought create connection to the power of your higher self. The higher self has qualities of absolute knowledge, absolute love, absolute happiness and absolute potential. The more connection you have with your higher self, through meditation and extended periods of no thought in your daily life, the more happiness and love you feel, the more wisdom you will have and the more power you are able to access in order to create the life you truly desire.

2. To create the life you desire, you firstly contemplate the life you would truly like to live. This should be done by alternating between thought and no thought, or in other words, between your worldly self and connection to your higher self. Once you are certain of what you want your life to be like, you then write these goals or intentions down in detail, as described earlier in the book.

3. Read these intentions or goals just prior to meditating. By remaining non-attached to the results you are creating out of happiness, not out of fear or out of the ego. You are not attached to the results for your happiness as you already feel true happiness now.

4. By putting your present moment attention on that which you intend, you as your worldly self are acting as co-creator with your higher self to take present moment effective action to help manifest or create that which you wish to appear in your life situation. Intention is for the future, attention is the present moment action you take towards the intention manifesting into your life situation.

Chapter 12

෴

A Magical Life of Happiness and Effortless Success

Through the process of awakening from the dream of thought you are able to start effortlessly attracting the circumstances into your life that you truly desire. Although the vast majority of our society have yet to start the awakening process, there are an increasing number of people who have and the number of awakened people is starting to grow.

An awakened person lives in the flow of life with a background feeling of joy and happiness and they create their lives from a position of happiness and *not* fear or too much attachment to things. Success is easily attracted to them in whatever they wish to do or achieve whether it be business, sport, relationships or family life. As they go about their daily lives they do so out of a feeling of background happiness and therefore help bring happiness to people around them. They are also able to see our society as it truly is with all its ego conditioning and structures. They are able to understand the motives and fears of people, being able to see why people do what they do and act as they act.

They are able to see how people are the result of their conditioning by society, their parents and circumstances and therefore do not judge too harshly, knowing them to be thinking and acting, not fully out of true choice, but out of past and present conditioning. They are able to see the truths of the world and how it really works. As they have started to let go of their own past conditioning and judgments they do not see the world or others through a distorted veil of existing conditioning and judgments but are more able to see society, people and circumstances in this world as they truly are.

They also find it easier to foresee undesirable circumstances and therefore more easily remain clear or free of them by taking appropriate action or non-action as is required in the present. They are able to feel what a person is actually thinking when talking with them. They do this not just by what the person is saying but more importantly by listening to their own higher self which is known as intuition. They do so this by paying full attention to the other person, listening not just with their senses but also with their higher self.

They are therefore able to more truly communicate with others as they let go of their own past conditioning and judgments and are able to know and respond to what the other person is really saying. The decisions and actions they take are intended to be the best ones to manifest happiness for them and for every one affected by their decisions and actions. They feel a connection or unity at a deeper level, beyond ego, to other people even when they do not personally know them and also towards animals and nature.

They realize that at the level of their higher self they are connected with all living beings and nature. They feel an underlying inner sense of peace and happiness and the actions and activities they do in this world are initiated and done out of happiness and not out of fear. Although they have an intention for things to happen they do not force anything. They just go with the flow of life and know things will happen when they are meant to. They do not think too much about the past or future but predominantly have their attention in the present moment of no thought or present moment action. When they do think they are mostly thinking about the positives of their life.

As humans we are all on the learning journey of life together. An awakened person is no different. They will still experience the flux and change that is life on earth. They will still experience loss of loved ones and other challenging situations. Natural variations in energy levels and surface mood will still therefore occur. These natural rhythms are part of the human experience. However through a connection to the higher self a deeper level of happiness and knowing is maintained throughout the surface level ups and downs that is characteristic of life here on earth.

Moreover as an awakened person maintains a stronger connection to the higher self the natural ups and downs of life have less and less effect on the enduring happiness they experience. As further transformation starts to take place, life even on the level of the worldly self, appears to have increasingly fewer lows or problems. A greater feeling of constant happiness both on the level of the worldly self in addition to the deeper higher self is the amazing result.

When a problem or challenge occurs the awakened person will firstly accept it and will not resist it. Once they have accepted it they will take responsibility for the situation, not blaming others or themselves for it but just knowing that things are as they are. This does not mean they will not deal with the challenge or problem. In fact they will, but in a detached manner.

Once they have accepted the situation they will listen to their higher self for the answer by alternating between thought and no thought. This is the worldly self and higher self working in conjunction. If action is needed it is taken. A creative solution which does not need force will appear. An awakened person also knows that in any problem or challenge there is also an opportunity for growth.

They will know that the more you give the more you receive. This does not necessarily mean giving away money or objects. It means giving people your full attention, a smile, a compliment or perhaps helping them in some way. It means fully accepting a person and not judging them.

As you give so shall you receive.

They know that the easiest and quickest way to receive something is to *firstly* give it. For example, if they want love they firstly give love, if they want respect they firstly show respect and if they want friends they are often the first to be friendly when encountering others.

They know that the amount of money that is attracted to them is in relation to how much they are helping others to get what they want, whether it be a product, service or information that others desire. They therefore know that to attract money to themselves they need to provide something that is wanted and needed first, whether it be through the supplying of a good product, a service or information. They know that what they attract into their lives is not necessarily what they want but is a result of what they put their attention on. The objects, people and circumstances that they put their attention on appear more and more in their life and conversely if their attention is taken away from these things then they will tend to disappear from their life. They know that in order to attract anything they want in their life they follow in one way or another the universal secrets or laws that have now been revealed to you.

Chapter 13

Eight Spiritual Secrets of Good Health

The mind and body are connected. The mind can affect the body and the body can affect the mind. The mind can affect the body in a number of ways. The more someone is strongly in their ego the more they will tend to suffer from minor or major physical ailments, depending on the extent to which they are in their ego along with the length of time they remain in their ego.

Over time someone who is strongly in their ego will tend to suffer more from physical ailments than someone who is less in their ego. Those people who have agitated minds will tend to have more agitated or sick bodies. Disconnection from the higher self results in feelings of separation and fear as people and situations are deemed as more threatening. The result is tension of the mind, which produces tension throughout the body and restricts the flow of life force and energy.

Therefore the way to enjoy better general health is to have a calmer mind and to feel more happiness in oneself. As you feel on the inside, so you will tend to feel on the outside, in your body. Happiness on the inside tends to result in good physical health. However unhappiness within will result over time in a variety of different physical ailments and poor physical health. The poor physical health can subsequently make an individual feel worse inside, resulting in a negative self-perpetuating circle of unhappiness and poor health for the individual.

Good Health

As you read and incorporate the secrets of happiness explained throughout this book you will tend to find that your general health improves over time. Generally speaking, the happier you are the healthier you are and the healthier you are the easier it is to feel the happiness inside, producing a positive self-perpetuating circle of happiness and health.

It is commonly known that continuous stress and worry results over time in poor health. Our natural state is one of good general health, however as the conditioning, demands and expectations of our society start to take hold our minds become more agitated through thinking and worrying.

The more we have our full attention only on the forms in this world, either on physical forms or thoughts, the more our life energy or consciousness is attached to them, which results in less life energy and consciousness within our bodies. The more we live our lives through the ego and the more we are constantly thinking the more our life energy within our bodies becomes depleted. The more the life force present in our bodies is depleted over time the more our health will suffer.

The following are ways in which you can help yourself increase the level of good health you experience.

Longer Periods of Connection to Ones Higher Self

The longer the period of connection to ones higher self the healthier a person will generally be. In other words the more happiness you feel within the healthier you will tend to be.

Plenty of Deep Sleep

Whilst you are in deep sleep you are connected to the universal consciousness which helps restore the life energy within you that has been depleted during your waking day. A good night's sleep helps to create a healthy body. You will know that when people are ill they tend to sleep more. Deep sleep restores the life energy in the body which helps heal illnesses and helps maintain good general health.

Non-Attachment to Present Physical Ailments or Health Problems

If you are already suffering from a physical ailment or poor health it is better *not* to dwell on it. The more you dwell on it the more it will tend to persist. As you give it attention you are giving the ailment part of your life energy that will tend to make it persist and remain.

The more you are able to take your attention away from thinking about the ailment the less pain and suffering you will tend to experience and the more likely it will begin to disappear. On the other hand the more attachment you have to your health problems the more they will stick around. The more you worry about present health problems the more they will persist.

To help you heal a health problem firstly fully accept the situation without judgment, that is to say do *not* think 'I have this pain and I shouldn't have it' or 'I wish that I didn't have this pain' as this is judging it. Instead say to yourself *I have this health issue and accept without judgment it is present. Following acceptance you choose to have a detached intention for it to disappear.* This allows some space to appear around the pain or health issue, which firstly gives you some relief through detachment from the pain and secondly allows healing a chance to take place.

To help detach further from your health issues or pain practice meditation, which works by removing your attention away from the pain during the meditation period. In addition to this you can say positive suggestions to yourself prior to the meditation such as *I am naturally healthy and I am now starting to return to my natural state of good health.*

Detached Observation of a Pain or Health Issue

From the position of your higher self, that is no thought, observe the pain in a detached manner without judgment. Just as one can observe other forms without labeling them or thinking, you can also do this with the pain or health issue you may be experiencing. *Observe the pain without thinking and without judgment and then let it go.* It can also be helpful, after you observe the pain in a detached manner, to say to it *relax and let go or relax and be healed.*

The Manner of Thoughts Concerning Your Health

Many people who have a particular pain or health issue understandably are quite regularly aware of the pain and this awareness results in the mind connecting to the pain. For example with regard to shoulder pain someone may regularly say to themselves "My shoulder is really hurting, I wish it wasn't but I don't know what to do about it and it is really getting me down". The more someone says the above to himself or herself the longer it will take for the pain to go, for it to be healed. So if you are unable to take your attention away from the pain you can instead choose to say to yourself "I am aware of a sensation in my shoulder at present, however I am sure it will disappear as soon as I let it go or as soon as I start thinking about something else".

Remember what we discussed earlier in the book, at the level of your worldly self, as you think so you are. So if you are constantly thinking about health problems they will become a part of who your worldly self appears to be. *Think of yourself as being healthy instead.*

Healthy Food and Drink

In addition to restoring our life energy through deep sleep and through connection to our higher self, we can also help to replenish our life energy within our bodies through food and drink. The more natural a food or drink is the more benefit we will receive by consuming it, as the more life energy there is within it. The definition of natural food with regard to this is that which *has not been processed* and which does not contain unnatural preservatives, additives or flavorings. Examples of natural foods are fresh fruit, fresh meat, fresh fish, fresh eggs, fresh vegetables and plain nuts. The most natural drink is of course water, which also helps to flush toxins out of the body.

The more the type of food you eat is in its natural state before you eat it or cook it, if it requires cooking, the more life energy it will contain and the better you will feel as a result. Conversely the more processed and junk food you eat the worse you will feel and over time and this will tend to be reflected in an increased number of ailments. Listen to your body's reaction to different foods that you eat. If a certain food tends to make you feel unwell consider eliminating it from your diet for a while. By eating and drinking more healthily you will feel better on the inside which will be reflected on the outside through better general health.

Physical Exercise

Light to moderate physical exercise helps you to stay in shape. As you exercise you stay in shape physically and therefore put less stress on your organs and joints through excessive weight gain. Also as you exercise your attention is taken away from your mind and into your body. As your attention moves away from the mind you start to think less or stop thinking altogether, your life energy within your body then increases, which is reflected in the general health of your body and a good feeling inside.

As you exercise the mind starts to quieten and you start to connect to your life energy within your body. Following exercise this good feeling can stay with you for some time, especially if you are able to continue having extended periods of no thought when not exercising. Light to moderate exercise can therefore help you to have a healthy body and a healthy mind.

Dance

Dance as a way of feeling and expressing joy has been practiced in all cultures throughout the ages and is also practiced in many celebrations and ceremonies. Dancing as a physical exercise can be particularly helpful to people. In addition to the benefits that the physical exercise brings you also experience benefits of the music.

Many forms of music carry a high vibration frequency within them as they are created when the music writer is in a creative state of no thinking and connected to their higher self. The music that is created therefore carries within it an energy that vibrates at a higher level. As we dance to the music we can move further towards our higher self as we move in rhythm to the energy of the music.

Chapter 14

From Chronic Pain to
Good Health –
My Miraculous Journey

As you may have previously read in the section *About the Author* I suffered from chronic pain from the age of fifteen until the age of forty. I was a very competitive child and by my teens increasingly felt the pressure, worry and stress of competing in this world. I suffered in relative silence to begin with but the pain kept increasing. I saw a number of doctors and specialists from my mid twenties into my thirties, however none were able to offer any cure and strong prescription painkillers were prescribed.

I was eventually diagnosed in my early thirties as having *atypical facial pain* of which the cause was unknown. It expressed itself as a neuralgia type of pain in most of the whole left hand side of my face. The pain was constant and started on waking in the morning and persisted throughout the day varying in intensity from moderate to extreme in a ratio of approximately 50-50. When the pain was severe it felt like a hot poker being pushed into the upper orbital bone of the left eye, or into the left jaw socket or both at the same time.

As the doctors and specialists I had been seeing were unable to ascertain either a cause or a cure I was eventually referred to a pain specialist. I was offered the option of having the nerve to the left hand side of my face cut, but advised that even this may not stop the pain. Although the surgery would render the left hand side of my face totally numb, the doctor advised that I may still experience major discomfort because of the total numbness, and may also still experience the chronic pain in a similar way that someone who has a painful limb amputated can still continue to feel the pain.

I therefore decided *not* to pursue the surgery and was instead prescribed an extra painkilling drug resulting in a total of ten tablets to be taken each day. The ten prescription tablets that I took helped to reduce the pain to a certain extent but also caused me to feel chronically tired. The only temporary relief I had from the pain at the time was either during physical exercise, relaxing in a sauna or when I was asleep.

It was not until about a decade later in April 2002 aged forty when real healing began. My approach to life had started to change approximately twelve months earlier, the catalyst being the news that my father had been diagnosed with a terminal illness and we were told that he probably had only about two years to live.

I had started to question the things I considered to be important and the way I thought about things. Importantly I began to slowly become less self centered, less selfish and less in my ego as a result of the concern I felt for my father and also because of the effects his terminal diagnosis had on my mother and brother.

I was lying in bed in the early hours of one morning, drowsy but not asleep. I was feeling particularly low as the painkillers that had reduced the pain to a certain extent over the last ten years no longer seemed to have any effect whatsoever. The pain appeared to be as bad as it ever had been despite taking ten prescription tablets each day.

It was then that *an answer suddenly came to me, seemingly from nowhere. The answer seemed so true and so strong that I jolted upright in bed*. The solution was to stop taking one of the drugs completely which reduced the number of tablets I took each day from ten to two. *Looking back I now know that this answer came from my higher self*, which of course has pure knowledge. However at the time I was not aware of this and could not understand, from the limited perspective of my ego mind, how this could work, as surely the pain would get even worse if I stopped taking one of the two separate drugs I was on. I also knew that to stop taking prescribed medication abruptly could be dangerous and that I would also probably suffer withdrawal symptoms.

Despite these concerns *the answer that had come to me felt so true and so right that I took action the very next day*. I stopped taking one of the two different painkilling drugs I was on. The result was an immediate increase of energy. Looking back I now realize the drugs were somehow reducing the connection I had to my own life force and as the connection increased I felt more energy and the pain began to disappear.

The immediate effect was a reduction in the amount of time I experienced pain from approximately eighty percent to ten percent of the time. This lingering pain stayed with me for several months until I received a second message from my higher self with regard to *the letting go of the remaining pain.*

The message I realized was just that, *to let go.* I realized that I had *always* been thinking about the pain prior to the times I experienced it. I may have been thinking about it one hour prior to the pain occurring, or twenty four hours before or somewhere in between. The message I received, *to let the pain go* was to *stop thinking and to stop remembering the pain.*

I now realize that as I remembered the pain and thought about it I was giving the pain life energy and therefore re-creating it. *The challenge was to stop remembering the pain, to stop thinking about it and to let it go.* At that time I had not fully developed the ability to stop thinking whenever I chose to and therefore at regular intervals my ego mind would remember the pain. This would happen every few days and I would experience the pain either later on that day or the following day.

The solution, I realized, was that in order to let it go I must first try to stop remembering and thinking about the pain as this was causing it to re-appear. Secondly if it did appear, to just observe the pain in my face in a detached way and to say to the pain, *relax and let go.*

The key to this was to accept the pain first and not to resist it, then to observe it from a position of no thought. In other words if the pain appeared I would become more present and create a stronger connection to my higher self. With the strong connection to my higher self I would observe the pain in a detached manner and then say to it, *relax and let go. Amazingly this always worked and within a few weeks the pain disappeared completely.*

As previously explained I had already stopped taking one of the two pain-killing drugs which had reduced my daily pain relief tablets from ten to two. Now that I was no longer experiencing the pain I reduced the other drug from two tablets to one a day and continued to be *pain free*. I subsequently felt a further increase in energy levels and was feeeling *no pain for the first time in over twenty five years.* I did not however wish to stop taking the final tablet as I thought the pain might re-appear.

The decision however to stop taking the final tablet was made for me two years later, when the pharmaceutical company decided to suddenly stop manufacturing the drug! My doctor informed me of this and I had no option but to stop taking it. I subsequently suffered withdrawal symptoms following the abrupt way that I had stopped taking the final tablet of the medication that I had been on for well over a decade, but *I remained pain free.*

The withdrawal symptoms disappeared after a number of months and for the first time in over twenty five years I was both *pain free* and *drug free.* I remain so to this day.

Chapter 15

❧

Life's Free Spiritual Gifts

You will probably be aware of the well known saying, *"The best things in life are free"*. This is true and I have included in this section a list of the simple things in life that can help you to connect to your higher self and therefore help you to feel more happiness, joy and love. These universal gifts help you to connect to your higher self by helping your energy frequency to change to a higher level than that of the ego mind.

Animals and Pets

Many people who have pets especially dogs will understand how much happiness their pet can give them. One of the reasons for this is that animals are generally speaking much less in their ego than humans. They live life much more in the present moment than humans and therefore have more of a connection to their universal nature and universal love.

Universal love is an unconditional love and this is what pet owners feel from their pets, especially dogs. Their pets tend to love them whatever happens. As pets live more for and in the present moment they tend to be more open with their love and joy and therefore when you return home, whether you have been out for a few minutes or all day, you receive an excitable loving greeting from your dog. Many pet owners feel a real connection to their pet and even feel that their pet can sense what they are feeling and thinking.

The reason for this is that the pet connects to the owner not just on the level of the mind but on the level of no mind, or in other words, on the level of universal consciousness which is beyond the thinking mind. Pets, especially dogs, can help humans to feel better as they make their owners feel loved and totally accepted for who they are without any type of judgments occurring. Because of this owners feel love towards their pets, which is of course returned with interest from their pets, and therefore there is a circle of love created between the pet and its owner. One way, therefore, to feel more happiness and love is to consider getting a pet.

Spending Time in Nature

By spending time in natural surroundings such as in the countryside, mountains, forest or by the sea people tend to feel better in themselves. They tend to feel calmer and more at peace and happier in themselves. The reason for this is that nature itself vibrates at a higher frequency that is beyond the thinking mind. Nature in the form of lakes, rivers, seas, countryside, mountains, plants and flowers does not have a thinking mind and therefore does not have an ego.

As it has no ego it is a purer expression of universal consciousness. As you spend time in nature looking at the beauty and listening to natural sounds such as running water, birds singing and leaves rustling this will help your mind to quieten. Your own energy vibrations will harmonize with nature's energy vibrations and subsequently you will start feeling a connection with both nature and your higher self. Therefore to feel more happiness, consider spending more time in natural environments.

Music and Art

There are some types of music that carry within them a high level of consciousness such as soul, classical, jazz, soulful pop and country music amongst others. The best of these contain music and sometimes lyrics that have been created whilst the music writer is *not* purely in their ego or thinking, but have come to them whilst they are *not* thinking. The music and the lyrics just come to the writer and are written down. The writer fluctuates between mind and no mind in order to write the composition.

The music therefore carries within it higher energy vibrations. As you listen to this music you can feel the universal energy or love within the music, which can then help you to connect to your higher self through the music.

True art can in a similar way help people to connect to their higher selves. The best works of art are created in the present moment whilst the artist is fully present and not thinking. Using the example of painting, universal consciousness and universal beauty expresses itself through the artist and into the painting. As you therefore look at and contemplate a painting, the painting itself can help you to experience and connect to universal consciousness and beauty through your higher self.

The painting itself has been created out of a connection with universal consciousness and therefore the beauty within it still carries a certain amount of the same energy. This energy within the painting helps your own energy field vibrate at a higher level, helping you to connect to your higher self as you contemplate the beauty of the painting.

The best works of art and music are therefore those that have been created whilst the artists themselves have had a strong connection to their own higher self. Therefore to feel more happiness, consider visiting art galleries and listening to uplifting music.

Water

It is well known that water can have relaxing and curative properties and this is reflected in the number of spa towns that sprang up over the centuries and which have dated back to roman times. Many people nowadays enjoy saunas, steam rooms, baths, showers or even just floating in water. The reason one feels a sense of well being whilst enjoying these activities is because they all help to take your attention away from outside forms, to inside your body, and therefore help you to connect to your life force within or in other words, your higher self.

In essence there is a movement away from your worldly self towards your higher self resulting in a feeling of peace, calm and well being. The more connected you are to your higher self the more likely ailments will disappear by themselves. This is one of the reasons that many people over the centuries have placed such an importance on the curative qualities of spas water.

Massage and Human Touch

The reason that massage can be very enjoyable is that again in the process of being massaged your attention is moved away from the outside world of forms, to your inner life energy within your body resulting in a feeling of contentment, well being and inner peace. In addition to your attention moving from outwards to inwards and the benefits this brings, during the process of massage there is also transference of life energy from the masseuse or masseur to the person being massaged which contributes further to a feeling of well being for the person being massaged.

Providing the person is performing the massage willingly with an open heart, they too will feel benefit from the giving of the massage and can enjoy an increased feeling of well being also. This is the result of the universal secret of giving and receiving as described earlier in the book, *As you give so you receive.*

In a similar way human touch in the form of cuddling or holding hands can also give a feeling of well being to both people. Using the example of cuddling, this takes your attention away from the world of form and into your body and therefore into your life energy. There is also a positive loop of giving and receiving life energy for both people. Both are giving to the other and at the same time also receiving it back, and due to the universal law of giving and receiving both people experience an increase in their feeling of well being, contentment and happiness.

Humor

Good-natured humor is a creative act and carries within it high energy vibrations, the energy of happiness, joy and laughter. Humor therefore helps people to feel good as the humor or joke releases positive energy and this energy is given outwards. People receive this energy which makes them feel relaxed and happy. Humor also helps people to come back to the present moment and away from the often negative thoughts of the mind relating to the past or the future.

Humor helps people feel good because it is an act of giving and receiving. The person being humorous is giving positive life energy which is received by the listener, making them feel good, and this energy is then reflected back to the initiator of the humor.

Humor in the form of sarcasm on the other hand comes from the ego self, and carries within it negative energy which shows itself in a form of attack. The purpose and energy behind sarcasm is negative and is intended to make the recipient feel bad. It is borne out of the ego and is a form of control and attack.

Observational humor can be particularly helpful for people when the humor is practical and presented with a positive energy. In addition to the positive benefits previously discussed, observational humor also has the added benefit of showing how crazy and silly certain situations which we regularly encounter in our ego based and conditioned society can be. As such it helps teach the audience not to take life's situations too seriously, and helps us realize that we should also not take ourselves too seriously either.

So to feel better and to help others feel better consider a little good-natured humor as you go about your day. Or perhaps instead of watching the 'News' on TV, consider watching a comedy. Ones that cause you to laugh out loud can help you to feel particularly happy. Some of the ones I find myself laughing out loud to are classics such as Laurel and Hardy, Rising Damp, Dad's Army and The Simpsons.

Chapter 16

❧

A Wonderful Life

People now more than ever are questioning what life is all about. *Why are we here? What is the purpose of life?*

I believe the purpose of life here on earth is twofold. The principle purpose is to awaken from the ego mind and to realize and remember who we truly are. *Who are you?* At the level of your higher or true self you are part of universal consciousness, eternal and perfect, a part of the divine. You are a spiritual being of divine essence that has manifested for a time here on earth in physical form to experience, encounter, love and share. The principle purpose of life is therefore to remember who we truly are, to experience and see life through our higher selves which in turn opens our eyes to the beauty, joy and love all around.

The main purpose of this book is to help *you* the reader to awaken. Awakening to realizing who you truly are is the process of disentwining the higher self, the eternal and true you, from the ego or worldly self.

It is the process of disentwining thoughts and awareness. It is the journey from the ego self towards the higher self. The longer we take to awaken the more suffering we will experience. Whilst we remain only in our ego selves we suffer because we are cut off from who we truly are. Prior to awakening, our divine essence is fully entwined with our thinking mind, resulting in a temporary forgetfulness of who we truly are. By maintaining a connection to our higher selves, and through our higher selves to universal consciousness, to the divine, we start to remember who we truly are.

The second and subsequent purpose is to *live and create our lives here on earth* through a continual connection to our higher selves and through our higher selves to the universal consciousness or the divine. To live and create in happiness and love, with a connection to our higher and true self. The stronger your connection is to your higher self the easier and happier your life will be. Increasingly you will start to live in the flow of life, to be at one with life. You are part of universal consciousness or the divine which wants for you what you want for yourself and that is happiness and abundance in everything.

As you begin to experience life more from the perspective of your higher self, more as the observer or watcher of your worldly self, worldly situations and objects, you start seeing life in a totally different way. You start to truly see and feel the beauty and love all around. As you live and create your life more and more from this connection to your higher self you will not only experience a wonderful life for yourself but will also touch the lives of others and access the power to manifest your desires.

By maintaining a connection to your true self and the power you enjoy through this connection, and its connection to universal consciousness, you are able to create the life you truly desire with ease. As more and more people begin to experience their true selves the world will begin to transform for everybody, transform into the beautiful and happy place it is destined to be.

Remember that life is a journey and occasionally we all stumble along the way. Whilst we reside here on earth we are all human and as humans we are not perfect. As we travel along the path towards increasingly experiencing our true selves there will be times when life situations and others successfully draw us into our egos and we find ourselves being too attached to a challenging situation or person which results in worry and suffering. When this happens be easy on yourself and know that these times will happen less and less as you patiently travel the path from living purely in the ego towards developing a sustained connection to your higher self.

The secrets to manifesting worldly success have been revealed to you in this book and as you start to live more and more from a connection to your higher self your power to manifest will continue to increase. Remember your happiness does not rely on what happens outside of you but on how you interpret and react to it. As you change on the inside so does your life as you are experiencing it. You will then find that the outer world is a reflection of your inner you, a reflection of your thoughts, attitudes and beliefs. Once you are able to control your thoughts you are able to control how, when and what you think about and this is reflected or manifested sooner or later into your outer world. In this world, so you think, so you are, so is your world.

Remember that true happiness is experienced when you have the strongest connection to your higher self, when you are the watcher or observer, your attention is within and you are not thinking. If you spend most of the time connected to your higher self and when needed alternate between thought and no thought you will find happiness both within and without. You will be able to manifest the life situation you have always wanted, simply by intending it and subsequently taking the effortless action that you will know to take.

Throughout the course of this book the spiritual secrets of happiness, health and success have been revealed to you. Once you have felt the happiness and peace of your true self you will never look back.

The final ingredient is your own free will to now choose to start living and practicing these truths as you go about your daily life. *The rewards for you are truly beyond words.*

THANK YOU

☙

If you have found this book to have been helpful I would be grateful if you would please share this with me by posting a *five star review* on www.amazon.com. You can do this easily by firstly finding *The Spiritual Secrets of Happiness Health and Success* by Andrew C. Walton on Amazon, then by clicking on customer reviews and then clicking on *Create your own review*.

On the same page, at the top right below *Wish list*, there is also a free Amazon *Share with Friends* email service for sharing this book with Friends and Family.

☙

RECOMMENDED RESOURCES
☙

A Course in Miracles by Dr. Helen Schucman. (Foundation for Inner Peace, 2007)

The Divine Matrix by Gregg Braden. (Hay House, 2008)

The Prophet by Kahlil Gibran. (Laurier, 2003)

Tao Te Ching, The Definitive Edition by Lao Tzu – translation by Jonathon Star. (Penguin, 2003)

The Way to Love by Anthony De Mello. (Image, 1995)

Printed in Great Britain
by Amazon